Small Steps
on Paws and Hooves
A Highland Journey

D TALBOT-PONSONBY

SMALL STEPS WITH PAWS AND HOOVES

This edition published 2010

First published in 1998 as *Small Steps with Heavy Hooves*
Second edition published in 2001

Copyright © Spud Talbot-Ponsonby 1998

Summersdale Publishers Ltd
46 West Street
Chichester
West Sussex
PO19 1RP
UK

www.summersdale.com

Printed and bound in Great Britain

ISBN: 978-1-84953-043-9

*For everyone whose life has been affected by cancer...
and for their children.*

Acknowledgements

My thanks go to everyone who looked after us during the Grampian trip, especially the Gammack family; Simon at Invercauld; Rob's Mum and Dad; Bea at Invermark; Eric and Cathy; Jim at the Drovers Inn; Frances at Peel Farm; the proprietor of the Bridge of Cally Hotel; Dick and Marjorie at West Gormack. Also thanks to Philip at Lee Valley Saddlery.

Thank you to everyone who donated money to the charities (Maggie's Centre, NSPCC and Children 1st). The total raised was £3,600.

A big thank you goes to Sophie, for her companionship, good humour and perspective.

Thanks from my heart go to all the people who ultimately made the trip possible, to everyone who rallied around when I was pregnant and after the cancer diagnosis, especially the Scott-Watson family for giving me love and enormous support from the time I moved to their farm; the Hughes family, especially Madge; Fiona for being the best 'birth partner'; Jo, Sue, Gail and Gaynor for their invaluable friendships, my GP for catching the cancer early and the doctors and consultants who treated me, especially Eunice the ward Sister; the Macmillan nurses for funding Susan; Susan for looking after us all; Marion for being there; everyone at Maggie's Centre; Ffyona Campbell for saying the right things at the right time; the many other friends and family who kept me going – thank you.

My love and thanks go to the people closest to me, though distance doesn't always make it easy: my sisters Charles and PC who dropped everything and came to be brilliant when I was ill; my other sister, Poopa, who was there in spirit if not in person and who gave me the recuperating holiday in the Seychelles; my unique father, Pops, whose hand I reach out for still; and lastly Rob, for his endless patience, love and encouragement during the cancer ordeal, the Grampian trip and the writing of this book.

Thank you Tess and Ben, two great friends.

Thank you to Barnie, the greatest gift.

World Health Organisation's definition of health:

'A state of complete physical, mental and social well-being and not merely the absence of disease or infirmity.'

'God grant me the Serenity to accept the things I cannot change, Courage to change the things I can, and Wisdom to know the difference.'

Reinhold Niebuhr

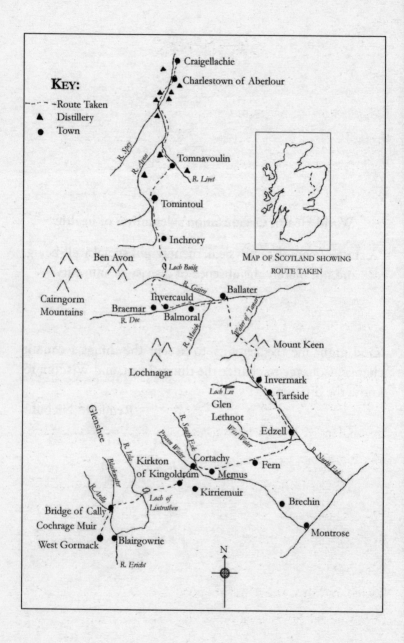

KEY:
- - - - Route Taken
▲ Distillery
● Town

Craigellachie
Charlestown of Aberlour

R. Spey
R. Avon

Tomnavoulin
R. Livet

Tomintoul

Inchrory

Ben Avon

Loch Builg

Cairngorm
Mountains

R. Gairn

Ballater

Invercauld

Braemar
R. Dee
Balmoral

R. Muick

Water of Tanar

MAP OF SCOTLAND SHOWING
ROUTE TAKEN

Mount Keen

Lochnagar

Invermark

Loch Lee
Tarfside

Glen
Lethnot

West Water
Edzell

Glenshee

R. Isla

Prosen Water

R. South Esk

Kirkton
of Kingoldrum

Cortachy

Memus

Fern

R. North Esk

Blackwater

*Loch of
Lintrathen*

Kirriemuir

Brechin

R. Ardle

Bridge of Cally
Cochrage Muir
West Gormack

Blairgowrie

R. Ericht

Montrose

N

Contents

Foreword

Everyone has their own way with coping with the obstacles that life throws in their path. Some events are more difficult to come to terms with than others – being diagnosed as having cancer is one of them.

Spud was a single mother living in the Scottish Borders and was diagnosed with cancer when her son, Barnie, was only four months old. After undergoing a hysterectomy to remove the cancer – as well as any hope that she would ever have more children – Spud attempted to come to terms with the emotional and physical scars left by the disease.

As an avid walker who had already walked round the entire coastline of mainland Britain (4,500 miles), Spud's natural means of attempting to come to terms with the changes taking place in her life was to go on a walk. However, this was no ordinary walk but a remarkable journey with her 'unorthodox' family following the old Scottish drove roads, steeped in history and whisky, across the Grampian Mountains of northeast Scotland. Entwined with the delightful travelogue is the story of a much harder journey. Often funny, sometimes sad but always disarmingly honest, Spud describes the events that brought her on this Highland journey. Anyone who has suffered from cancer, or knows someone who has, will be able to relate to the enormous effect that the disease can have on your life – the fear, the taboo, the uncertainty of the future, the resolutions. Having fought cancer myself, and made a comeback to racing fitness, I can relate to the intensity of that feeling. *Small Steps* is much more than a travel book. It is a book that should be read by mothers as well as anyone who has suffered illness or has been through difficult times. Spud's brave and insightful account of this 'walk back to health' will give entertainment, comfort and inspiration to many.

Bob Champion

Preface

In July 1994 I stood on Tower Bridge in an euphoric moment of achievement. I had joined a select band of people who have walked the entire length of Britain's coast, and respect showed in the eyes of those around me. I thought I had undertaken the journey of a lifetime. How wrong I was. Two years later I became pregnant, was left by the father, gave birth to my son and, four months later, was diagnosed with cancer. These events were to take me on an emotional journey which involved more pain, tears and fatigue than walking Britain's coast ever could. In an effort to come to terms with all this, I did what felt best and went for a walk. In September 1997 my family and I undertook a journey of catharsis across the Grampian mountain range. Before the reader goes any further, my family, described by some as 'unorthodox', needs some clarification.

The Family

The first confusion arises because my dog is called Tess, I am called Spud, and everyone thinks it should be the other way around. To overcome this, we have become each other's alter ego and share names accordingly. But remember: Tess is the one with four legs, a tail and no inhibitions.

On 23 June 1996 Tess and I were joined by Barnaby Benjamin. His father had long since decided to jump pregnancy, and Tess became surrogate sibling and part-time baby-sitter. Four weeks later Ben the horse arrived, and the boys were soon sharing names as frequently as Tess and I.

Then came Rob, the only person willing and able to take on the family in all its muddle. Miraculously he seems to have clung on to his name, at least for the time being.

The Journeys

Barnie was riding before he could walk. Where other eleven-month-old children rode in buggies, Barnie was strapped into a wicker basket saddle atop Ben and accompanied us on walks in this manner. I had discovered a freedom not available with your average buggy. The Scottish Highlands beckoned.

In September 1997, Barnie, Ben, Tess, Rob and I drove north to Aberlour (on Speyside). The plan was to walk southwards through the Grampians, following old drove roads where possible, with the aim of getting as far south as we could. Barnie rode Ben, who also carried all our food and camping equipment.

This book tells the story of the 150-mile, three week journey from Aberlour to Blairgowrie. But it also tells the other story; the series of events which led to the Highland trip – of single motherhood and coping with cancer.

Not all physical travel takes you to desirable destinations, and so it is with emotional travel. Some destinations are exotic, some are hard work, many are humbling, most are memorable, all are valuable. The intensity of feeling my own journey evoked took me by surprise and made me appreciate the remarkable journeys that every one of us undertake as part of what we call life.

PREFACE

This is not a travel book in the strict sense; but I am writing this book because I know now that the destination doesn't have to be exclusive to be memorable or fulfilling. I also feel that positive things can come from my experiences and, if they do, then the journey will have been worthwhile.

NB: The events of the Highland trip were recorded on a dictaphone. I usually spoke into the dictaphone several times a day; as we were walking along, when we stopped for lunch, and at the end of the day. These ramblings have been transcribed and edited to form this book, but remain in the sequence that they were recorded.

Swimming With Dolphins

Every time I looked up, I saw the dolphin. It was leaping out of the water displaying enormous energy with no apparent effort; caught on camera to become a poster to adorn the labour room of the Borders General Hospital. I envied its weightlessness. I felt about as weightless as a tank in a quagmire.

'Come on. You're nearly there,' encouraged Margaret, the midwife. 'Get that little Spud out.'

I laughed – painfully, politely. But my eyes were drawn back to the photo, and this time I felt the first overwhelming surge of love for the life struggling to enter the world.

'I'm going to take my baby swimming with dolphins,' I declared with complete, drug-induced conviction.

'Yes, yes,' soothed my two companions, failing to hide the fact that they didn't believe me, or didn't care, or both. Yet it was suddenly so vitally, vitally important to me. I would take this baby swimming with dolphins – maybe not just yet, but soon. I knew then that I wanted to share my life with this person, and to show him or her the world – which was lucky really because there was certainly no going back.

Encouraging me through the birth was Fiona, mother of one and now five months pregnant with number two.

'You must have a 'birth partner' everyone had said to me, single mother-to-be. I was sceptical, wallowing in my bed of self infliction. So embedded was my belief that I could overcome all things alone that I had no need for such modern terms. Besides, it sounded a little like needing a waltzing partner when you have flat feet, no co-ordination and no rhythm.

The only partner I required was the father, sitting on the ceiling rafters with a length of string around his testicles. This is how the Huichol Indians share childbirth. Every time the woman has a contraction she pulls the string, thus ensuring that the father feels adequate pain too. It sounded like a pretty good idea to me.

Now I was swallowing my scepticism. Only another woman can possibly understand this extraordinary, animalistic, nightmarish, euphoric moment in a woman's life. Childbirth brings you closer to your animal origins than a woman will ever experience. I was out there, in the jungle, under a thunderous sky, howling and panting in unison with all the other creatures of the universe. For one glorious moment we were bonded by this common thread – so primeval, so strong, that it enables a pumpkin to emerge from a hole the size of an egg.

Childbirth is the point of no return; like taking off in an aeroplane, knowing that you can never stop until you reach your destination. Telling the pilot to stop mid point over the Atlantic is simply not possible.

'I can't do it,' I suddenly blurted, tears threatening. My pilots were stern.

'You can. You're so nearly there. PUSH!'

I thought there would be blood and tears when the thing finally emerged but there weren't. There were two legs and two arms and this doughy, bap-like body rolled in flour. Two blue eyes looked at me with shock. All was quiet.

Overtaken by instinct, I pointed him in the direction of a boob. He sucked instantly. The amazing instinctive behaviour of migration became less of a marvel in those minutes. Some things just happen.

'Meet Barnaby Benjamin,' I said, looking up at Fiona (who was luckily still five months pregnant and had tears rolling down her face). I had clearly forgotten my one promise; never to burden my children with names as long as mine. Twenty-nine letters simply do not fit on to the average bureaucratic form, but this wasn't something I thought of as I held my son for the first time. Oh well. He could shorten it to BB and become a blues singer or an author.

Barnaby Benjamin weighed in at 9lb 2oz and was soon stripped of his innocence by being wrapped in a Babygro and placed in a perspex goldfish bowl. We had left the jungle, never to return.

Fiona disappeared and I was left to sit in a bath and come to terms with things.

Until now I had told myself that the biggest drawback to being single had been the inability to reach my toenails during pregnancy. I had ripped several sheets, and, not having lived in the area long, I knew few people well enough to ask them to perform this task.

I had become very good at seeing the advantages of my situation. There was no one to moan about early morning *insomnia when I would rise with the dawn to make tea and toast, and sit watching the sun warm the ripening corn outside the window. There was no one to tell me that I shouldn't drink coffee, or smoke that cigarette, or eat that blue cheese. There was no one to argue with over names, and no reluctant partner dragged along to the antenatal class to sit picking his fingernails or staring at his boots. There was no one who wanted meals at conventional times, or minded feasts of avocado and garlic roulé. There was no one to complain about the garlic.*

I reminded myself constantly of these things. When I heard other pregnant women complain about mother-in-laws, husband's washing, arguments, indecisions; or when I heard mothers' complaints of pissed fathers, elusive fathers, unable-to-put-a-nappy-on fathers – I felt smugly happy with my situation, as though I was eating a great big sticky toffee pudding all on my own. Occasionally, just occasionally, people said 'lucky you'. That crowned the sticky toffee pudding with an enormous dollop of fresh cream.

Unfortunately that was only one side of the story. The truth was, I didn't want to be on my own. Despite what some believed, I had always envisaged myself taking the more conventional route. Getting married, settling down, then having kids. Lots of them.

Barnaby was the result of a passionate summer affair with a stonemason from Stoke. This sounds like the subject of a romantic novel – except that a subject is no good without a plot.

I knew I was pregnant almost immediately. The father was ecstatic. We discussed genders and names, and wet the unsuspecting baby's head with numerous bubbles. Then the plot dried up and the father dropped me from a height. The landing was hard and rocky.

I did what felt best and cushioned my fall with alcohol. It was autumn, and I was trying to write a book about my round Britain coastal walk while house sitting an empty cottage in the bottom of a dark valley in Devon. The steep valley walls hid me from the rest of the world, and it from me. I curled myself up in front of the fire and howled. No one heard.

I tried following the father's example, but running away from yourself is never so easy. Down here, in this deep pit full of demons which taunted and jeered, I had meetings with myself at every turn.

At times when I managed to chase the demons away, I saw the clear river of my instincts. I had been down the termination road before, and vowed never again. But even vows have minds of their own. At other times I came face to face with my values. I didn't want to take this life. The pregnancy was the result of one night; was this fate?

Society was the demon which swept all others away. The lower I sank, the louder was its collective voice. It wouldn't approve.

Damn society, this is my life.

Is it? There are two of you now.

My life. My instinct. My decision.

But can you cope?

The arguments raged like the autumn storms.

The stream on which the cottage sat was prone to flooding. One night there was a particularly big storm and the stream levels were rising. I went to the garage and found the sandbags as instructed. Some were rotten and fell away in my hands, but there were, at least, sufficient to block the door.

I blocked myself in and went back to the fire. The stream thundered by outside the door, and the alcohol thundered around in my head. Blood and water were one and the same thing and I saw then that I was on the road to nowhere. Following the father's example would never work. I couldn't run away from myself. I had two options, and knew, had always known, which road to take.

The storm had passed in the morning and I noticed that an acorn, gathered from my favourite thinking spot and placed casually on the side in the kitchen, had produced a brilliant white shoot which searched vainly for water and nutrients on the plastic surface. It was symbolic enough to reaffirm my decision – the most important one I would make in my life. You cannot turn away someone whom you love very much, and haven't seen for years, just because it is an inopportune time.

One of my sisters said I was brave to make such a decision; but I knew that it would have taken more bravery to choose the other route. That decision would have haunted me forever.

Decision-making is tormenting in itself. I knew that things wouldn't be easy, but being happy with myself meant that at least there would never be any blame. Blame is the scapegoat for so many 'wrong' decisions. At least now I could restart my life. I planted the acorn in a small pot and took it with me to a rented cottage in the Scottish Borders, where I finished the book and began a new chapter.

I held my stomach in until I could hold it no longer, and celebrated my pregnancy privately. It might have been the 1990s, but pregnancy was still taboo. It reminded me of the time after the death of my mother; people consciously tried not talking about mothers, which meant they talked about them even more. Now, everyone talked about single mothers, remembered me, and shut up. No one congratulated me on my pregnancy. Instead, there were embarrassed, awkward moments, and pregnant pauses in the literal sense. I was staggered. It bothered others more than me. I had made my decision.

None of this stopped me craving warmth and care from someone who loved me; which is why, as I upended myself in the coal bunker during that cold winter, or felt hungry slabs of loneliness engulf me, I reminded myself of the advantages... no alcohol-saturated, vomiting partner to chauffeur home 'because you really shouldn't drink darling'... no one to loll in the bath when I wanted one... no one to tell me I was doing too much, too little, too fast or too slow... no one to... I climbed out of the bath and went to the ward. When morning came it revealed a ward full of Rhonas and Ians and Stewarts and Douglas's. There were McKenzies and McGregors and McPhersons – in fact, a cocktail of clan names who, over the years, would have been happier shedding each other's blood rather than comparing births. Into this fearsome band, like a peasant to the clan chiefs, was thrown Barnaby Benjamin Talbot-Ponsonby.

Everyone peered at Barnaby's name card and said, politely, that they liked the name; but it was clear from their faces that I may just as well have called him Epidural.

But Barnaby had done his best and had a fine smattering of ginger hair. With that, and a few blasts of Scottish liquid sun, he would soon pass for a Scot. I imagined him in years to come, kilt clad and whisky-cheeked, saying such things as 'ye dinnae ken, lassie,' and being teased down the pub for being named after his great-grandmother, Barnabine. Would he ever forgive me?

Breakfast appeared. It was two Weetabix and a thin handkerchief of Mother's Pride. I wolfed the Weetabix and went in search of the toaster to cheer up the despondent Pride.

'Have you had a Section?' came the extraordinary response when I enquired about a toaster.

'Umm. No.'

'Well, you can't have toast then,' the nurse told me as though she had been practising this one line all night. 'Only those who've had Sections can have toast.'

I carried the sad bread back to my bed, vaguely considering that it might have been worth having a Caesarean just to be allowed toast. I ate the bread with a small packet of jam, and still felt ravenous. Was I supposed to produce milk from two Weetabix and a flannel of bread? It occurred to me that, in farming terms, it wouldn't be long before I was 'milking off my back' at this rate.

As that June morning progressed into hospital day, the fathers of Ian, Hamish etc., began to flock into the ward. I sat alone in my bed looking expectantly at the door. I wasn't sure who to expect, but surely someone was telepathic?

I finally geared my sore self into action and went to the telephone. Hospital rules said that only dads were allowed to come and go at any time of the day, which is pretty bad luck if dad lives miles away, doesn't know you've just given birth, and doesn't give a fig anyway. A nice nurse (not the one in charge of the toaster) said I could nominate another person. I chose the closest I have to a mother, Virginia.

Like all new mothers, I wanted to show off my handsome son to the world. He was beautiful, calm, quiet, serene. In short, he was everything all the other babies in the ward weren't. It is amazing what maternal instincts do to one's perspective. Where there were blemishes, I saw only perfection. Where there was disquiet, I saw only harmony. I was like a bloke with a new car, desperately wanting to put Barnaby through his paces in front of a watching world.

Forty-eight hours without toast was enough. My sister, Charles, appeared like a saint and took us back to our farm cottage, bathed today in the usually shy Scottish sun. Tess was waiting at the door and shot out like a thunderbolt to welcome the new arrival. This four year old, temporarily under-exercised bull-terrier-cross-village-dog, the equivalent, I imagine, of hyperactive twin toddlers, saw competition for my affections.

By way of introduction, Tess the toddler manoeuvred herself on to my lap and introduced Barnaby to his first taste of halitosis. 'How developed are a baby's nasal passages?' I wondered, guessing that at two days old Barnaby was unable to distinguish between Colgate Ultra and Rotten Rabbit.

Nasal passages aside, Tess was soon showing me the efficient method of what the midwives had described as 'topping and tailing' your baby – and displaying a definite preference for the tailing. Nevertheless, acceptance was acceptance.

The big wide world, and the excitement of meeting his hairy sister, triggered Barnaby's appetite. Time for some boob; Barnaby on one, and Tess, intrigued by the smell of milk, aiming for the other with a row of canine teeth.

Settled at last, a warm glow enveloped me. My happy family, I thought, until – scratch – Tess' toenails made contact with Barnaby's head. He bawled.

Was I supposed to recognise this rendition among a room full of screaming babies? Where instinct was apparent at times, it was non-existent at others. Oh well. It was enough to recognise a bark from a cry; and enough to kiss better the long white claw mark across Barnaby's head, and, for the first time in my life, know what it is really like to make someone better.

I was overwhelmed by my instinct to love and protect this little person. I would have killed for him, swum in the Arctic Sea on Christmas Day – even gone potholing for him. The feeling wrenched at my heart, pulling it from its cage and engulfing Barnaby – thus bridging the physical gap between us.

I felt whole.

Where in the World is Aberlour?

Friday 6 September. Waiting for Rob.

Charlestown of Aberlour lies on the northern fringe of the Grampian mountains, fifteen miles inland from the Moray Firth. It belonged to the Laird of Carron, who had two sons – Archie and Charles. Clearly Charles was favourite, because he was given the thriving town on the River Spey while poor old Archie was given a measly village two miles away. Archiestown should perhaps be renamed Archiesvillage – though I guess it doesn't have quite the same ring to it.

We arrived in Aberlour yesterday afternoon having loaded Ben into the transport lorry first thing in the morning. Ahead of him was the six hour journey to Aberlour. But he didn't know if he was going five minutes down the road, or across the country to carry Barnie over the Grampian Mountains. For all he knew he could have been en route to Pennsylvania, yet he wouldn't have blinked an eyelid if he had driven for ten hours and arrived back in his field at home.

27

It appears to be the lucky lot of babies and animals that they live for the present. The past may ring small bells in the mind of a horse or dog (possibly called selective memory, depending on what is at stake); but the future appears to have no meaning. It is the here and now which is important.

Half an hour later I loaded Tess and Barnie into the car, and set off northwards after Ben. They accepted the situation with the same blind trust. Tess might have sulked at the fact that she was squeezed into a pocket-sized space, and possibly wondered why it had taken days rather than hours to pack up, but she asked no questions. Before long the pair of them were asleep and I was left to my thoughts.

When Tess and I walked Britain's coastline, Tess loved to stop and linger over the vinegary remnants of every chip newspaper, or to take up the challenge of a chocolate wrapper moulded on to the pavement by a hundred holiday feet, or to take joy in a single pebble on an empty beach. When I called her on, reminding her that we still had so many thousands of miles to walk, she would look at me without comprehension. If I had walked and walked and walked, she would have followed me until she dropped.

Such is the warm glow of trust which animals and babies give us, and which it is our privilege to receive. It certainly brings out all the mother hen instincts in me.

So when does a baby lose such a philosophy? His mother is always hurrying him on; finish that meal, put on that coat, leave that gloriously muddy puddle. We are going to the shops, the library, out to lunch. And when that is done we have to get back. Slowly, but inevitably, time becomes indoctrinated, and we set our children out on the rush which is life.

Ahead of us now are three weeks of walking, and it is pretty hard to rush when you are walking. Some people may power walk to take vigorous exercise, but Ben is a one paced, six-year-old Clydesdale X Cob. He is Clydesdale in all but height and is, precisely, one horse-power. Certainly no more, and frequently less, depending on the wind, the terrain, and his state of mind.

It is good to be here, on our own, knowing that the way home relies on the placid bay horse in the cemetery field. One horse power suits me just fine. But why are we really here?

Ten months ago, when Barnie was five months old, I had an operation to remove cervical cancer. Naturally it took time to recover from the operation physically, but it is taking even longer to recover from the psychological impact that cancer has on every aspect of one's life. I wallowed in a bog of 'Why me?'s for months, until the idea for this trip came to me like a strong hand reaching to pluck me from quicksand.

When Tess and I walked Britain's coast, I discovered a deep contentment brought on by the world close by and the simplicity of life on the road; where so many daily trappings are shed and the air that you breathe and the ground which you tread become important. So, in an effort to come to terms with the past eighteen months of my life, I planned this journey of catharsis. It is, perhaps, an attempt to rediscover that contentment.

Barnie, Ben, Tess and I are here, waiting for Rob to arrive tonight so that tomorrow we can set off to walk southwards through the Grampians. Escape? Possibly. I don't really mind what people call it. We are here, and anticipation hangs in the air like droplets of mist which never settle. It is sensory, not tangible, reawakening a distant memory of health and strength.

It is late afternoon and we are sitting looking over the River Spey to where Aberlour is shrouded by trees. Fifteen month old Barnie is just learning to walk and is doing his impression of one who has sampled too much Speyside Malt Whisky – a few staggering steps, then falls to the ground.

Undaunted, he picks himself up and tries again. They say that, because whisky breathes while maturing, a good deal evaporates (the 'angel's share!') – possibly as much as four million gallons per year in Scotland (lucky angels). This may also explain Barnie's behaviour.

Within a one mile radius of Aberlour, I can count five distilleries marked on the OS map. Within a five mile radius I can count roughly sixteen. It is hardly surprising that the air here is saturated with the yeasty smell of malting barley. It hangs over the peaty brown water of the Spey so that one permeates the other. You get the feeling that the Spey is the aorta of the area, the life-giving vessel – which indeed it is when you realise that the livelihood of the area depends on its flow.

Distilling stops during the summer months because the water level is too low, and to allow the stills to be cleaned. Never mind that this is the season when people flock to the area to witness the whisky process. Whisky isn't a tourist attraction, but business – big business. It is one of Britain's top five export items.

Aberlour's other business is fishing. The river bank today is littered with serious men and women dressed in camouflage clothing spending mega-bucks to catch the mother of all salmon. In fact, I'm sure any salmon would do. Why is it that you never ever witness a fisherman catching a fish? Of course, they'll tell you that the water was too high, too low, too fast, too slow, too clear, too murky, too wet, too dry.

Yet Aberlour doesn't have the feel of a town made ritzy by fishing. There aren't rows of shops selling tweeds, fluorescent flies and socks at £15 a throw; and the high street isn't shadowed by four wheel drives adorned with rods and fishy mascots. I haven't even seen a single dusty, stuffed fish declaring 'fifty pounder caught in the exclusive £800-a-day-pool' in a single pub, shop, house or museum.

Aberlour is a no-nonsense town constructed of purposeful granite. Granite has a determined air; square, neat and precise like a pristine and frighteningly conscientious school matron. Each block is large and foreboding, a cathedral in itself. I wouldn't like to mess with granite.

This morning I picked up a town map of Aberlour from the empty Tourist Information Centre. Our first port of call was the small village store next door; but if it's a tin of beans you're after, forget this store. Unless you want a tin dated 1950.

The store is now a museum. Everything which sat on the shelves when the store shut in the fifties remains; pickled, preserved, and displayed on and in beautiful wooden counters and shelves as a wonderful glimpse into the past. I chatted conspiratorially into my dictaphone as we went around the shop:

'The Challenge Artificial Silk Blouse. Knicker elastic – threaded ready for use – extra strong. Flasks used by distillery workers to steal whisky from the still, strapped to the chest under the shirt. Maids' and nurses' caps and aprons. Phantom Pure Silk Stockings. Big hardback music books, faded and dusty. Would they ever produce them in this throw away society? Wringers and mangles and churners...'

The store is clearly still a shop of sorts, and the lady in charge appeared reluctant to talk but keen to sell. However, I needed neither knicker elastic nor maids' aprons, and it was difficult to know what to buy without attempting to offer money for some priceless artefact, the only one of its type still in existence. I thought also of Ben, who will have to carry everything from now on.

Opting for safety, I bought Barnie a book. We had decided that, like us, he would be allowed one book and one book only on the trip – but more for our sanity than for his, I purchased another here. *Hairy Maclary of Donaldson's Dairy* will see us through to... well, wherever we get to.

Scuttling out of the shop just as Barnie was beginning to whine on my back, and retrieving Tess from a lamp post, I perused the map again.

Marked at the far end of town was 'Walkers Shortbread Shop'. I pictured a small family-run home baking enterprise (aimed, presumably, at walkers of the Speyside Way) which served real coffee and shortbread straight out of the oven. My mouth watered at the thought of the buttery biscuits melting on the tongue, so we set off up the High Street. Geared for walkers, I presumed that it would cater for dogs and babies alike – thus leaving me to rest my legs and enjoy coffee and shortbread in peace. Well, no one had told me that *the* Walkers Shortbread was produced in Aberlour.

'It's at the end of town, in the industrial estate,' the girl on the street informed me after I had peered hopefully into every small doorway expecting to see my cosy shop. 'You can't miss it. It's huge.'

My vision was shattered when I looked up and saw the large factory complete with steam and a clinical sign pointing in the direction of the Visitor's Entrance. Instead of being welcomed by an ample bosomed woman with floury hands and a cheery face, we were virtually run over by a ten ton truck, then a forklift.

Walkers Shortbread is still, however, a family run business. It was started by Joseph Walker in 1898, whose ambition it was to produce the finest shortbread and oatcakes in the world. The company is now run by his three grandchildren and has become the largest independent biscuit manufacturer in the UK. One glance at a service station gift shelf, or visit to an airport duty free shop, and the familiar tartan packaging of Walkers Shortbread will back up this statistic. Walkers has become a symbol of Scotland in more than fifty countries. The bulk of Walkers products are still produced here, in Aberlour.

'But we have another enterprise in Elgin,' the shop lady told me. 'They mainly produce low fat biscuits,' which seemed a contradiction in terms to me. Surely the reason we eat biscuits is to taste the butter and sugar and feel that warm feeling of wickedness?

I bought a big bag of broken shortbread, and one of oatcakes, and left the shop munching on these. Barnie peered over my shoulder, dropping buttery crumbs down my back while Tess picked up the rest as we made our way to the orphanage.

Things seem to be coming together, as they often do; as though this whole venture was meant to involve Aberlour. Visiting Aberlour Orphanage had fixated itself in my mind as some sort of homage.

I have Barnie to thank for being here in many different ways. This 'thing', this whole mad year of mine, all started with the unplanned conception of Barnie. Could I, would I, have ever been able to place my 'unwanted' child into such care? If we were living in Victorian times... The day became a pilgrimage.

Aberlour Orphanage was founded in 1875 by an Anglican clergyman, Rev. Charles Jupp. This was a time of Victorian consciousness and philanthropy, and Jupp came to Aberlour from Newcastle in search of cleaner air and better health. He was, apparently, an outspoken character who vociferously criticised the existing treatment of orphan children.

Many children weren't necessarily orphans. Some had been abandoned by parents, while others were, of course, illegitimate. The children who came to the orphanage were from all walks of life, all social classes, and Jupp appears to have been a kind and determined fellow who ran the orphanage on a shoestring. He made the children's clothes and would be seen knitting socks on the train.

The orphanage was closed down in 1967 – the year I was born. All that remains is the clock tower which stands forlornly hemmed in by a housing estate; pebbledash houses, stained paling fences, stained glass windows, shiny lamp posts and paving stones. All perfect, all immaculate – except that the clock had stopped. I felt let down and betrayed by the presence of it. I couldn't even find a plaque explaining the tower's presence.

Barnie sat under the tower, picking up pebbles from the gravel driveway and scattering them over the swept paving stones. He was so happy, yet so small and slight and vulnerable. Is it really possible that society could have *made* me put Barnie into an orphanage?

Aberlour pays tribute to the orphans who once lived here in other ways. In the village store/museum a book lies open to be signed by anyone who was once here as an orphan, or relatives of residents of the orphanage. A steady trickle of people return through the years, to see the remaining walls which were once their home, and to witness the stopped clock.

Last night, the landlady of the pub also made reference to the many many people who return to Aberlour to seek their 'roots'. It seems an odd combination of people who visit Aberlour; orphans, fishermen, shortbread connoisseurs and whisky lovers.

To my delight I have discovered that the pub caters very well for children; highchairs, high teas, and high enough tables so that I am not constantly rescuing salt shakers and vinegar bottles. The landlady has a ferocious face masking a gentle nature and within minutes, last night, she had found several toys for young Barnie, clearly feeling sorry for this child who has been dragged across the country only to be expected to ride half the way home on a horse. We were two of only a handful of customers, which may have helped too.

The pub is a matter of paces from our bed and breakfast, which is run by the Gammack family. Six weeks ago we came up here on a recce trip to discover whether certain routes were feasible for Ben, and to find him a field for these initial two nights. We were drawn to 'C. A. Gammack – Saddler', and Charlie took us under his wing.

Gammack's Saddlers is the pulse of Aberlour. You have only to stand outside the shop to meet Aberlour (and witness the endless stream of whisky tankers rattling by, temporarily turning Aberlour from cosy village to busy highway).

The saddlery shop itself sells anything and everything. It is a den to browse in, yet nothing compared to the enormous garage at the back where Charlie hoards his real treasures. This is a feast to the eyes of any would-be saddler or craftsperson; tools and screws of every size, rolls of leather, rolls of canvas, old pack saddles, ancient but indestructible sewing machines. Charlie once made harnesses for the army – we are staying with the right person. He has offered to inspect our very home-made saddle pack arrangement tomorrow.

Leaving Charlie's treasure trove via the door behind the counter, you enter the world of Mrs Gammack and the B&B. Our hostess is petite, efficient, and takes her role of wife seriously. Her eyes brim over with an enthusiasm which flows out and is evenly spread around the present company. It would be impossible to feel apathy in her company.

I am enjoying the transition from customer to resident to friend. There is something heart-warming about seeing life behind a shop, and to witness scenes of domesticity once the 'closed' sign goes up. It is just one of many reasons for bemoaning the arrival of superstores. At least they will never mend saddlery.

We took Ben out this morning. His field is no more than three hundred yards from the B&B, and borders the cemetery on one side and a rather precious garden on the other. That is, a precious garden minus a few shrub branches now making their way through the vast stomach of dear Ben.

I thought Ben might have been wary of the new surroundings and strange, malty smells here, but he walked easily off the lorry ramp yesterday, narrowly missing two Aberlour ladies deep in conversation who never expected to meet a hulk of a horse on the pavement. He had shared the trip here with two Falabellas (the smallest breed of horse in the world) en route for Skye. They were being met halfway by a mini bus in which to complete their journey.

Far from being overawed, Ben appears to be taking all this in his stride. He continues to grab hold of my sweatshirt, or the back pack, or anything else he can get hold of and take security from, but that's nothing new. My one concern is always that he might grab Barnie's hand. Crunch and gone. The thought repeatedly disturbs me, as I duck and dive to saddle up Ben while Barnie is hoisted on to my back.

I acquired the first wicker saddle when Barnie was under a year old. It was found at an auction by a friend, and had been loved and used over many years. Worms had made cosy homes with en suite rooms in the wicker, and the weak wire frame was stretched to its limit around the drum belly of Ben. It lasted long enough to realise I was on to something, and I went in search of someone to make a new one.

A local weaver put me on to the Scottish Basket Weavers Association who put me on to a guy in Norfolk who makes such saddles for Riding for the Disabled. I drew him pictures with precise measurements and stipulations, and within a month this beautiful brand new basket saddle arrived for the princely sum of £40. It was then a matter of getting a local saddler to attach straps for the girth, and various 'D' rings for the breast plate (to stop the saddle slipping back). I sewed thick upholsterer's foam on to the bottom, and attached the child harness on to the back. With a little bending and moulding, the new saddle fitted perfectly, and Barnie took up his position like a young Maharajah on his elephant.

'Doo... da... doo,' Barnie chants in anticipation as I saddle Ben. He loves being in the saddle, from where the view is magnificent and the rocking motion calming. After six months, riding a horse is as natural to him as riding in a buggy. A buggy is only slightly more predictable.

Ben strode out this morning. We went up the High Street a little, then branched away from the Spey to follow the Burn of Aberlour out of town. Here, the old granite buildings are replaced with new bungalows, and space is plentiful. Large concrete driveways, courtyards and sweeping gateways declare affluence, as do patios, columns, verandas and archways. These are not low cost houses.

Individual pine trees guard gateways and these, added to an intermittent smell of drains, gave the small road a continental feel. For a moment I was transported to the Algarve – until I noticed that several houses had signs offering the names of the residents. We passed 'Rosemary and Geoff ', 'Bill and Marjorie', and 'Fiona and Brian'.

We climbed the hill past these houses, admiring the hills which rose up to the south and east and accompanied by fields full of horses and ponies which kept Ben moving forward. Barnie pointed to each and every one exclaiming, 'Tesssss.' So far, he thinks anything with four legs and fur is a Tess.

We turned left at a junction, near yet another distillery, and came back along a farm track which ran through some birch woodland. The leaves are just beginning to change and the wind was sending the select few on a jive to earth. Some became caught in Ben's mane and I decided that, if I ever get married, I want autumnal birch leaves instead of confetti.

As we entered Aberlour again, we came past the Fleming Cottage Hospital. A plaque above the door said that it was founded in 1900 by Joseph Fleming, distiller and bank agent. Perhaps it is also thanks to Joseph Fleming that the Lour Hotel occupies the same building as the Clydesdale Bank? Would such cohabitation occur in England I wonder?

I like Aberlour.

The Start of Droving

Saturday 7 September

Rob arrived late last night. Barnie has a streaming cold, as do the clouds which smother Aberlour – neither of which makes us feel like moving today. I am relieved to postpone departure, although part of me is frustrated. I suppose I want to be on the road, to see if this journey is actually possible, and to postpone departure even once makes me think 'will we ever?'

I take a small step back. Cancer has a way of refocusing your mind and your life. Initially you want to do everything yesterday, in the fear that you may not be around tomorrow, but I am slowly learning to push away such drive and relax. Tess, Ben and Barnie are the wise ones. It is the here and now which is important, and I am pleased that we have postponed departure. This is, after all, my journey of catharsis.

This will be my time out from the world and all we have inflicted on ourselves. Time without phones, mail, health worries, hospitals, doctors (there's one doctor I can't shake off who has insisted on coming with us!).

I need to live with the land and the elements. I want to hear the rain close by and see the birds when they sing; and to know when the wind's in the south or the north or the west. I want to go to bed when it gets dark, wake when it gets light, and watch the clouds as they roll across the land, unhampered by buildings or artificial light. I want to appreciate the food I eat, the water I drink, the shelter I have, and the bed I take for granted at home. I want to know what it means to drive a car, or to turn on a light. And, above all, I want to do all this with the people I love.

Selfish? Perhaps.

I can hear the childhood mantra, '"I want" never gets'. Replace 'I want' with 'I would like' and perhaps people won't think so badly of me. Besides, I feel that I've worked to reach this point, to be able to say 'I want' and not feel so bad. Added to this is the fact that we are fund-raising, and fund-raising undoubtedly allows mad people like me to do mad things like this. Only this time, Barnie is suffering my insanity too.

Poor Barnie. His nose is streaming like a burn in spate. But cold or no cold, rain or no rain, Rob hoisted him on to his back this afternoon. I made some makeshift reins and clambered bareback aboard a very wet Ben, and we set off north along the River Spey to Craigellachie.

It felt wrong to be walking north because I knew that from here we should only be getting closer to home, not further away. As usual, Tess was oblivious. The sea on our right, the sea on our left; north, south – it makes no odds.

Craigellachie lies two miles north of Aberlour and was the point at which we originally planned to start the walk.

We are intending to follow original drove roads south, and Craigellachie was the gathering point where the farmers brought the cattle to be delivered into the hands of the drovers.

So who were the drovers? The drovers were what transport lorries are now. They were burly, hirsute Highlanders who drove their beasts through the hills and glens to reach the various markets.

At the height of droving, in the first decades of the nineteenth century, sheep and cattle were driven in equal numbers. The introduction of sheep came with the Highland Clearances; for centuries before, cattle alone were the mainstay and currency of life in the Highlands. For a long time the cattle trade was on a 'help-yourself-and-fight-if-you-get-caught' basis; wars were waged over them, and lives were frequently lost in defending them. Then, as the cattle trade became recognised and legalised, formal markets emerged – Crieff and Falkirk being the largest ones.

There is evidence that droving existed as early as the fourteenth century, and was certainly in existence in the sixteenth century. However, it was during the seventeenth century that lawless cattle driving evolved into lawful cattle droving; and the men who were once reivers (cattle thieves) became law abiding drovers – well, almost.

Even when droving had become legal, the Highlanders often preferred to roam the back glens and trade there – away from taxes and tolls and dues. Raids and forays between glens had been going on for so long that they were part of the Highland psyche. Acts of Parliament meant nothing; besides, no one could enforce such laws when they couldn't even find the men or beasts. The reivers and drovers knew the hills and glens like no one else did or probably ever will, and they came to illustrate and represent the Highlanders' tenacity and love of adventure. Over the years, the reivers and drovers have been romanticised in Scottish art and literature. Even Hollywood has been wooed by drovers.

These days it is harder to be adventurous – at least adventurous in your work. It is this combination of adventure and work which has made me fascinated by the drovers in a jealous way. My interest began with the drovers of Australia several years ago, where flat dusty tracks which shimmer in endless mirage and blue heeler cattle dogs set the scene. In the high lands of Europe too the drovers existed, and still exist, where transport lorries are unavailable or uneconomical and markets are close. *Transhumance* is the practice of bringing livestock from high summer pastures to winter pastures nearer the dwellings – this too is droving. Imagine spending your life walking the country behind a herd of shaggy cattle, bleating merino sheep or Heidi cows with resonant bells, and getting paid for it?

Added to this is the draw of a restless character. Nomads, gypsies, drovers – they are all characters who live by the law of the land rather than the laws of inertia. It is easy to romanticise them, but who's going to deprive me a little romanticism? Some people are wooed by candlelit dinners, I am wooed by the open road.

But to call the routes by which the drovers crossed the country 'roads' is to visualise the country as it is now. These were not roads. At best they were tracks, also often used for communication, carrying coffins or transporting whisky.

Very often, though, the drovers had no such lines to follow. They had no compasses and navigated by instinct, rivers, the stars and the features on the land.

In attempting to discover some of the routes they took, we are using Haldane's *The Drove Roads of Scotland*. It was Haldane who brought us to Craigellachie, a gathering point for the drovers, but somehow we ended up in Aberlour. Well, it was thanks to a kind Aberlour doctor who had a field for Ben.

Even though this isn't an endurance trip as such, with strict rules that we must start somewhere and finish somewhere else, it felt wrong to start at Aberlour. So this wet trip to Craigellachie satisfied any pedantic tendencies. When we turned to retrace our steps back to Aberlour, it was the start of the trip. We're off!

The drovers followed the Spey valley south from Craigellachie. Of course, every other form of communication then followed their route – roads as we know them, and the railway line.

The railway line has long since closed, and in 1981 the Speyside Way footpath was opened along its route. It is a glorious cinder path flanked by birches and Scots pines and larches beginning to turn. Now and again these thin out to allow glimpses of the Spey with the stick-like figures of fishermen braving the rain. At lunch time, they hurry to the wooden fishermen's huts which remind me of beach huts. Instead of lilos and deckchairs adorning their steps, you see rods and waders. Instead of a windswept granny knitting with gnarled fingers, you see Jeremy Fisher men spinning huge yarns about the one which got away. The theme is the same: good British perseverance in the face of the elements.

We came up here six weeks ago to see whether the Speyside Way was feasible for the wok-sized feet of Ben. Poor Ben. He doesn't know what's in store. His more usual occupation is cart pulling; now he is packhorse.

We discovered then that the track is easily good enough for him. The only problem we foresaw were the narrow stiles. The stiles are only a foot and a half high, but I don't think we'd ever persuade Ben to leave *terra firma* for that length of time. Ben walks through things, not over them, even without the weight of his packs. Luckily, the Speyside Way Ranger has agreed to unlock the adjacent gates tomorrow and Monday.

Our rough aim is to reach the original market (or 'tryst' in drovers' jargon) at Crieff. How many miles away from here that seems. If we make half that distance I'll be ecstatic. So much depends on the weather. I'll be saying a prayer to the weather god tonight.

The Days Before Tractors

Sunday 8 September

The clouds disappeared and gave us a clear day. No more excuses. No more looking through windows or opening doors. What a strange thought! Along with this goes no more newspapers, radio, beds, hot water, china mugs. Everything we need is here, with us, strewn around on the grass or strapped on to Ben.

Charlie helped us saddle up and we were finally off. It was an unceremonious departure; especially when the first obstacle became apparent after only ten yards. Trying to fit Ben through one of the narrow gates is a little like threading a sewing needle with baler twine. This time there was a way around.

The tunnel of trees which is the Speyside Way led us quickly to a ford, then a series of wooden bridges. Ordinary enough obstacles, you might think, but for a six-year-old horse they are all potential dangers: is there a way through the trees? How deep is the water? Will the bridge hold me?

Ben's ears shot back and forth, hearing and sensing everything. He snorted and sniffed, his eyes intermittently flecked with fear. For security, he grabbed hold of the strap on the backpack I was carrying. Ben has placed all his trust in me and it is up to me to honour that trust.

We had left Aberlour at eleven, just as Barnie was ready to sleep, and it wasn't long before his helmeted head was nodding in time to Ben's stride. No amount of animal noises could keep him awake. Normally we will stop for him to sleep, but we had walked such a small distance that today we transferred him to Rob's back, where he stills sleeps quite happily.

'How does it feel to be walking again?' Rob asked, in relation to the coastal walk.

When Tess and I finished the coastal walk I decided there would never be another long walk. My legs and hips agreed. They had already carried me over 4,500 miles in ten months, a distance covered by most people over years, and I don't want to get crumbly joints before my time. I knew there would be shorter walks of no less interest, but I never foresaw walking the Grampians with my own son aboard a horse, and a doctor as company.

How different the coastal walk was! To start with I took walking for granted and walked with the ease and arrogance of someone of my years. Now I remember my satisfaction at walking to the end of the hospital ward, bent double and carrying that damn catheter bag like the shackle that it was, and telling myself that if I could walk 4,500 miles, I could jolly well walk to the end of the ward. I vowed that I would *never* take walking for granted again.

It feels great to be walking now. I enjoy the fact that we are walking from A to B and no matter how far we actually get on this trip, the start will be different from the finish. Distance isn't important. We are using walking as a form of transport, going where the route takes us – which isn't always through the most beautiful, scenic country. We won't cover the same section twice, or retrace our tracks at all. Every corner, every day, produces a new view or a new experience. (I wonder what the drovers would think of such vanities?)

Every step, every mile, is another step through life; through other people's lives and the shared experiences. I want to give Barnie, Tess and Ben the opportunity to experience such things and thereby make their lives the richer.

And Rob?

Rob has abandoned his stethoscope for an OS map and looks the better for it already. He is at his happiest roaming the hills, and I hope this trip will bring riches for him too.

Yet walking is almost secondary now. I am primarily in the role of mother hen – guiding my family through the country, seeing they are fed and happy and comfortable enough to continue. This is survival. Instead of distance worries, I have maternal worries – and weather worries.

Damned clouds. They are in hot pursuit of each other today, playing their game of tag, each one more threatening than the last. I know that the success or otherwise of this trip depends on Barnie enjoying himself, which in turn depends on the weather. It is a simple equation. My eyes turn constantly to the sky. I dread rain as I once dreaded blisters.

We have stopped for lunch after four miles. The ample, smooth lawns of the distillery at Carron were too much to resist, and Ben is on his tether chain doing a grand fertilising job. The distillery seems so empty. Only the malty smell and steam billowing from the chimney hint that whisky production is under way.

Such distilleries are now manned by as few as six or seven people. Often they are controlled from a central computer elsewhere – so that potentially they can be controlled by one man. It is eerie to see this factory, sprawling and huge, with no man in sight. We are a little nucleus in this empty cell.

Tess has rolled in something very smelly. I don't know where she thinks she's sleeping tonight. She loves picnics, as does Barnie. As far as they are concerned, lunch on the floor means a free-for-all. Tess runs off with a 'Ben carrot', and Barnie crawls off in hot pursuit. At the sight of a dropped crumb, Tess abandons the carrot to Barnie and rushes over to peck at crumbs. Holding Barnie still long enough to force some food down him is a battle. Cucumber is a bit of a winner at the moment, as are oatcakes and Primula, both of which look like works of art once they have been rolled along the distillery lawn.

Just when we want to sit and dream, Barnie wants to take vigorous exercise. He crawls when he wants to get somewhere fast, and walks when he feels adventurous or when Tess is nearby to act as a type of zimmer frame. Either way, one of us is constantly retrieving him. And someone called this a holiday?

*

'I've been a wild rover for many a year,
    And I've spent all my money on whisky and beer...'

Rob, now nicknamed Wal because of his floppy, canvas 'I'm Not British Or Anything' hat, and the same type worn by the 'Footrot Flats' character, has been teaching us this song. My memory isn't very good for lyrics, but I can remember the gist. This one is about a prodigal son returning home – and we've changed rover to drover. I wonder if the drovers sung songs, as they battled through rough ground, following the meandering Spey with their tartan plaids swinging.

The Speyside Way was quite social. An American on a mountain bike sped past, then stopped for his sandwiches and we plodded by. Plod – I like that word. It sums up Ben. I saw Rob look a little enviously at the bike. He knows little about horses, and everything about bikes. We have an ongoing rivalry over whether two wheels or four legs are better. Personally, wheel wobble has always got the better of me.

Apart from the American, we passed several families who looked incredulously at Barnie perched up on his steed. Tess stole a stick from a young girl and produced tears, much to Barnie's amusement.

At Dalmunach, a farmer made a beeline for Ben.

'Isn't he magnificent? You don't see many of his type any more.'

Ben has a way of producing such nostalgia from those who remember life before tractors.

'We used heavy horses like this all the time,' he went on. 'Myself, I used to breed Highland ponies which were used to take coal round the distilleries.'

The farmer took hold of Ben, who was trying to decide on what to eat next, and you could immediately see that he had handled horses all his life.

'I'll stand no nonsense. Try your best, and I'll treat you fairly,' he said to Ben. Respect shone in Ben's eyes.

Reluctantly, the farmer went to leave us. He hoisted his tired body back over the fence with the help of a stick, and marvelled again and again at the sight we made. 'Grand horse, grand set up,' he muttered, clearly smiling within. Behind him we could see his farm with its usual melee of buildings and barns and bales. A couple of tractors stood where once there would have been horses.

Further on, another figure aided by a stick came into view ahead of us. He walked slowly, painfully. At the sight of us, recognition flashed across his face.

'Are you the ones walking to Crieff?' he enquired. 'I saw your leaflet in the window of the saddlers in Aberlour.'

The man shifted painfully. We were a good mile from any road access, and I couldn't help admiring the guy. He comes up here from Surrey every year and has been walking the Banffshire/Moray hills since 1943.

'You must be the doctor and part-time carpet-bagger,' he said to Rob, confusing Munro-bagger* with a rather less complimentary bagger of things. Apart from this, he had clearly read the leaflet well and was concerned by our declaration to live off the same diet as the drovers did – oatmeal, onions and whisky.

'Surely the little one won't survive on that? He'll get a terribly upset stomach, won't he?'

We reassured him that, though two out of three would certainly enter his diet, we would supplement it with other

*A Munro is a principal Scottish mountain over 3,000 feet. A Munro-bagger is a fanatic whose ambition it is to climb every one of the 277 peaks!

bits and pieces such as heather flavoured pasta and peat flavoured Primula.

From Carron the Spey meanders this way and that between its wooded drapes. Each and every name given to a farm or a hamlet sounds like a distillery; Culquoich, Tomlea, Dalvenuan, Toimintuigle. The area breathes whisky, so that it lingers in your hair and sticks in your nose. It would be impossible to dislike whisky in this area; it *is* the area.

Knockando really does have a distillery. We passed it after lunch, and yet again it was deserted. A row of flags were flying, though, and they were enough to set Ben off on a Clydesdale tango with himself, as the saddle bags slapped his side and made him spook more.

Poor old Barnie is like a rag doll on Ben and ended up slouched on his back in the saddle. As yet he has no comprehension of balancing himself. He looked startled, but then chided Ben from his recumbent position with an 'ah ah ahh…' as if to say, 'what the hell was that, you silly bugger?'

His resilience amazes even me sometimes. Rob and I laughed to remember one time when we were walking at home. We were deep in conversation when I turned to check Barnie – only to see no Barnie in the saddle. In fact, there wasn't even a saddle in sight. Ah… but there he was, slipped down to the side at a position below horizontal, almost between the plodding Ben's legs, and gazing at the world from this new angle as though such things were just meant to be. He didn't utter a squeak.

Situations like this remind me of Barnie's precarious situation. Ben is no Falabella, and Barnie's safety is the most important thing. If Ben is misbehaving at all, or the ground underfoot is rough, or we are on a busy road, Barnie rides on Rob's back instead.

We resurrected Barnie, as one might a capsized boat, and replaced the silk on his tiny helmet, which is not available in your average Mothercare, but was ordered from a saddler. Amazingly, this one, size 000½, is the second smallest available, suggesting there are those who start even younger than eleven months!

At Knockando we walked between the old station platforms, from which the whisky casks were once loaded on to the trains. On the scale of things, these railway lines had such a short existence. The platforms and stations are still evident and maintained to an extent; and we are camped tonight at the old Blacksboat Station.

The station is a lovely old stone building adorned only by its painted name board. Unrestrained by fences and unhampered by paths or gardens, the solid walls blend straight into the trees. As buildings go, it is free-range, more like an earthy rampart harmonising with its surroundings. It is hard to believe that it was built for anything other than aesthetic reasons.

Rob is busy working on passing his Pony Club D Test. He grooms Ben methodically and gently. It is clear that Ben will be the best groomed of all of us, and that is the way it should be. We are relying on Ben's good health and lack of saddle sores.

I was watching Ben graze earlier. There is nothing methodical about his grazing. He moves from one spot to the next at random, leaving behind good grass in search of the perfect patch, and it occurred to me that we are like that through life. We strive for a perfection which remains unattainable. When we have something, we want more. And when and if we have that, we want more again. There is no such thing as perfection because we will always want more. Perhaps the closest we will get to nirvana is accepting the here and now as the best option.

Buddhists practise mindfulness – the art of being able to fully appreciate what we are doing at that time; changing nappies and washing up in icy burns being no exceptions. Reaching such a state is hard, but something we should be striving for.

It is going to be interesting to live with Ben all the time. Normally he lives in a field and I have little idea of when he eats, sleeps, drinks or pees. I bought him fifteen months ago. He had come from Ireland, and I realise now that he must have lived in a city; while he never bats an eyelid at whisky tankers or shop awnings, he finds sheep spooky. There are two wandering aimlessly along the Speyside Way this evening. Perhaps they are in search of their drovers.

We are exhausted. But the tent is up, and the stove is heating water for pasta. If we get no further, we have walked and survived seven and a half miles. My doubting cousins from Hampshire will be impressed.

All for Luck

The countdown had started. According to the doctor I would become a mother in ten days time. I sat in the surgery waiting for my final check-up, delighted that my doctor ran perpetually late; the Health Centre was always warm, the chairs were comfortable, and, above all, it offered me an enforced escape from writing the book. I arrived early and found the most trashy magazines available.

I purposefully avoided articles such as 'How I coped with my toddler's tantrums', or 'In search of the perfect partner,' and usually opted for the travel pages. But now one article caught my eye – 'How to beat post-natal depression'. It read: 'After the birth of your baby, you may experience feelings of frustration and regret at the way your life has changed. It may feel as though your life is one continual stream of nappies, feeds and sleepless nights.'

Oh joy of joys to come! I thought, but read on with a morbid, morose fascination, as one might continue a terrifying horror novel (in the back of my mind believing, with all denial, that my baby would sleep well, feed regularly and be potty trained from the outset).

'You might be unable to see any other life apart from your baby,' the article went on. Then came the crucial sentence; 'Give yourself something to look forward to. Go out and treat yourself to something new, something you have always wanted. Do something which will make you feel good about yourself.'

At that moment the doctor called me in. He called 'Spud' rather tentatively up the corridor, much to the amazement of all the other waiting patients who possibly wondered if they had wandered into the fruit and vegetable market.

My doctor lived in a cottage on the same farm as me, and for this reason we had met socially. Outside the Health Centre, he had crossed the boundary from calling me Katherine in his best doctor's voice, to calling me Spud. But he still had problems with it within his professional capacity. He called 'Spud' then cowered, as though expecting to have rotten eggs thrown at him.

I had also registered that the doctor was uncomfortably young and good looking, but registering was all. I had been man-poisoned as one is food poisoned; I would be completely off them for a while, but, over time, would probably sample them again, possibly even get to enjoy them.

The doctor prodded my stomach, and was rewarded by a hefty kick from the babe. I was delighted that someone else had felt him/her kick. No one else had. But the doctor's hands were undoubtedly desensitised by the many kicks he had received over the years from angry, prodded babies.

I was sent off with an 'all's okay' and a 'good luck with the birth', and went back to finish the article on post natal depression. It wasn't that I necessarily thought I would get depressed, but until now the book had kept me busy and I realised that my solitary situation might only sink in after the birth of the baby and the actual publication of the book – which were both due at the same time. I left the Health Centre with one thought:

'I need a project. I need to realise the horse dream.'

You see, for as long as I remember (which admittedly wasn't very far back in those pregnant days), I had had this dream of setting off into the sunset in a gypsy wagon. The dream was gaining momentum, snowballing; now it had germinated and its roots were actually forming. I had found the perfect excuse.

The horse would be heavy enough to pull a cart, but small enough to ride and be easily managed. He would be young enough to start a life with me, but educated enough to be wise. Above all, he would be placid and a firm friend.

As luck would have it, I had recently been given the phone number of a guy near Carlisle who dealt in horses, especially driving horses. The minute I got home, I called Mr Mowbray.

'I've got just the thing in my yard,' came the reply to my enquiry. I fell silent. He was supposed to say 'I'll keep my eyes open, and call when I find something.'

As it was I fell prey and put the phone down smiling secretly. I had planned to go and see this 'perfect' horse the next week, six days before the baby was due; but I hadn't told the dealer to expect a gestating female who was already having Braxton Hicks contractions and could well go into labour during the hour and a half long drive to Carlisle, let alone while bouncing around on a rough cart behind a horse.

Of course, everyone thought I was mad. The article had been trying to tell the reader to go out and buy a new dress, have a haircut, buy a longed-for piece of furniture, have a massage – even buy a goldfish. A horse? A rocking horse for the child perhaps... but a real one?

I knew there was one person who wouldn't think me quite so mad. My would-be mother, Virginia, knew that it was pointless to dissuade me from an idea – so she joined me. Besides, anything which sniffs of horse will see her supporting the adventure. So we drove to Carlisle together.

Mr Mowbray wore a brown overall coat, a tie and a well-worn brown trilby which he touched in a gentlemanly fashion when we arrived. He looked at my bump; and in that look I saw neither speculation nor disapproval. I had grown so used to either one or the other that to meet a gaze of unconditional acceptance was to breathe a breath of fresh air after a long haul flight in the smoking section. I warmed to Mr Mowbray instantly.

Tied up to the fence in the yard was a collection of horses ranging from pony to hunter to fast fillies and coloured cobs, all standing silently, patiently. The bay gelding with the magnificent, hairy heels was the one we had come to see. I walked up to him and he sniffed my bump.

'He's only five, but he's as quiet as anything,' Mr Mowbray was by my side. 'He came from Ireland, where he pulled a cart for weddings. He was one of a pair, but he was too slow and got left behind. That's why he's being sold.'

I thought it was a sad tale. He was being sold because he was too slow. What sort of a life had he had? What sort of a journey had he had from Ireland? He must have experienced fear on the journey, and yet here he was still trusting and nuzzling.

I watched the horse being ridden and it was clear that he hadn't been ridden much; but once in the shafts, he was quite at home. I clambered on to the platform cart in an ungainly fashion, and we set off through the village. The baby turned several somersaults as we negotiated some vicious sleeping policemen, then settled down.

The bay ears flicked back and forth in front of us, responding to every utterance and encouragement from Mr Mowbray. Enclosed in the shafts, and tunnelled by blinkers, the bond between man and beast is at its most important when driving horses. Voice is everything. The voice must instil authority and confidence.

We passed children and vans and a busy village shop. We were overtaken by a lorry and a double-decker bus. The nameless bay horse flicked his ears, but never flinched. It was only then that Mr Mowbray made his confession:

'I haven't had him out in harness since he's been in my yard – since he came from Ireland.'

Yet he had taken this pregnant lady out and about... Such a display of trust was enough. I had found my horse, and discovered the ideal mode and pace to travel.

So far Mr Mowbray was dispelling every preconceived idea about horse dealers. There wasn't the merest whiff of falsity about him; no expected banter about this horse being 'everything you want' the 'best buy in town' the 'bargain you'll only find the once'. He was honest and direct, and almost seemed more concerned about where the horse would be going. He told me to go home and think about it.

The Braxton Hicks contractions came thick and fast on the way home; but I was several years down the track, renovating my wagon, packing up my child and all my possessions, and trotting off into the sunset behind the bay horse with the white legs and Clydesdale, feathery heels.

'You realise what a big commitment the horse will be,' Virginia cautioned, retrieving me from an idyllic, wooded lane and a meal of hedgerow ingredients cooked in a big cast iron pot.

I pointed to my balloon belly. 'And this isn't?' Virginia laughed.

'At least, if push comes to shove, I can sell the horse,' I said, and thought.

I phoned Mr Mowbray the next day to say I'd take the horse but that I didn't want him until a month after the birth. Could he keep him for me?

'Of course,' came the reply.

'What about money to graze him for the month?' I asked.

'Well, now, what you do is this,' Mr Mowbray said. 'You work out how much you'd give Mr Mowbray here for grazing for the month, but instead of giving it to me, you put it into a savings account for your child.'

If I had been face to face with my new friend I would have thrown my arms around him. His warmth of words and actions stayed with me for days, weeks, months; like the gently suffusing warmth from a log fire after a hefty blast of wintery air.

I gave birth to Barnie, and waited for the horse who had temporarily been named Hairy Heels. But when he walked *off the lorry ramp to begin his life with us, Mr Mowbray assured me that he was called Ben – which is a little like calling your dog Rover or Fido. I like it all the same, and, besides, it is bad luck to change the name of a horse or dog.*

'Talking of luck,' Mr Mowbray said over lunch of bread and cheese in our cottage, 'I'll give you this Luck Money.'

He took a ten pound note and a fifty pence coin out from his pocket. 'It's a tradition which dealers have when they sell a horse. It has to include a piece of silver, and is handed over to the purchaser in the wish that the animal will bring them luck.'

'I experienced this as a child,' Mr Mowbray went on. 'Nowadays the tradition is dying out, but the older dealers still do it. At one stage Luck Money accompanied the sale of any stock – cattle, sheep, any livestock.'

Mr Mowbray took out a pen and wrote on the ten pound note, 'Luck Money. R Mowbray 25 July 1996.'

'If you keep this Luck Money, you'll never be broke,' he said handing me the note and the coin. 'If you fall upon hard times you'll always have this.'

I assured Mr Mowbray that I would keep it forever.

'I sold a pony one day,' Mr Mowbray went on, 'and gave the lady a pound note for Luck Money. Twenty years later she phoned me up to say she was selling the pony, and would I take it. She brought it back to me, along with the same one pound note I had given her. I'll always remember that.'

Even Luck Money hasn't escaped inflation.

It is the fortuitous person who finds a kindred spirit on a dark night. Mr Mowbray's interpretations of life woke me from a dream, as though I had found a familiar face in a sea of strangers.

Where others were disbelieving in my dream to revert to horse transport, Mr Mowbray supports me to this day. He and his wife lived in a wagon until their second child was born and describes these days on the road as 'some of the happiest of our life'. He is a friend of the road and the people he meets along it, suffering no fools but embracing those who show willing. He seizes life with an open heart and both hands, and encourages those he meets to do the same. He has suffered hard times and good, and smiles through the peaks and the troughs as though recognising that it is such things which make us a whole.

Mr Mowbray was the first person to see the family I was creating, and the road I was taking. He made anything seem possible and when he left me that July day, I was a richer person. I may have been one thousand pounds poorer, but I had Luck Money, a lucky horse, and the blessing of someone I deeply respected.

It wasn't long before we were seen out and about as a family; Tess planning the route, me pushing the large maroon pram with suspension to make a John Deere tractor proud, Barnie's toes waving out at the summer sun from within, and Ben being dragged behind as one might take out a dog on a lead. No one had ever seen a horse being taken for a walk. In such a way we walked the lanes, discussing at length the dreams and plans we had for the future.

One day I was sitting bareback aboard Ben while waiting for the blacksmith. Barnie was asleep in the pram outside the cottage. When he awoke with a cry to demand a feed,

Ben instantly ceased his grazing and took me over to the pram. I was staggered and more than a little chuffed.

He then stuck his nose inside the pram and retrieved a blanket in his teeth – Ben's Linus blanket. Barnie's big eyes stared at the huge, hairy nose looming into his cocoon. The trio of Tess, Ben and Barnie were quickly getting to know each other. I felt that the Luck Money was beginning to work its magic.

A Taste of Cragganmore

Monday 9 September

I was 'on call' last night. One ear was constantly on Barnie, while the other was listening out for the ghostly dragging of Ben's tether chain – to make sure that he hadn't become tangled in it, and to make sure that he was still there. Before last night, he had only been tethered through the night three times.

Mr Mowbray taught me how to tether. In the beginning you fasten the fifteen foot chain to an old seat belt around the horse's neck, and let them drag this around the field. This teaches them how to step over the chain and get out of trouble on their own. Then you fasten the other end to a pin in the ground.

The first time I did this with Ben he became tangled and fell to the ground. The concept of being pinned to the ground was completely alien. From then on we had sessions every day, increasing the time he was tethered and helping him when he got into trouble. It was then time to tether him overnight.

One weekend we set off on a practice trip from my cottage in the Borders. We found a beautiful clover field in which to stop for the night, with magnificent views over the Tweed valley and back to the Cheviots. We set up the tent, tethered Ben, and settled down for an early night. But Ben was unused to this feeling of space, and was soon charging around on the end of his chain like an irate, chained circus bear. Eventually, the string securing the chain to the pin broke, and he was off across the darkening field dragging his chain – with me, clad in T-shirt, knickers and boots, and brandishing a carrot as though it was a claymore, in hot pursuit.

We repeated this ridiculous performance in the darkness several times until accepting that we were losing the battle, and deciding that Rob should go in search of a field. He set off on his mountain bike, with no lights, and along rough wooded tracks which he didn't know to some friends nearby.

Meanwhile, I hunkered down near Ben to try and talk some sense into him, thinking of people all over the country who were doing normal things on a Saturday night rather than being alone on a hill top with a baby and dog asleep in a tent, and a manic horse on the end of a chain. I also wondered how I had ended up with someone who was equally as accepting of such a hilarious situation. The only solution I came to was that we were both mad.

This conclusion was confirmed when Rob reappeared during the last hour of that day, muddy and puffing and distinctly dishevelled, by which time Ben and I had sorted out the world and he had settled down. It is hardly surprising that I am wary of Ben's night-time antics. I can see myself chasing him back along the Speyside Way, to Aberlour and to Charlie Gammack's doorstep.

The drovers knew what it was like to be 'on call'; they appointed a watchman every night. At the peak of droving in the eighteenth and nineteenth centuries, when towns had become too large to be fed by the country close by and railways had not yet provided a cheaper form of transport, the number of beasts passing from north to south in a drove could reach thousands. Such droves would stretch for miles across the Highlands. Sometimes the drovers had the luxury of dogs and ponies to facilitate their job, but usually they didn't. (Women and children would never have accompanied them.)

For every fifty or sixty cattle, there was one drover; and the whole drove was under the charge of the head drover, or 'topsman'. It was his responsibility to go on ahead, occasionally on horseback, and arrange grazing for the night and generally plan the route.

At night, however, it was the watchman who shouldered the responsibility. To keep guard of even five hundred wilful, loose cattle through the night makes listening out for the chain of one horse seem a breeze.

Although the cattle were tired at the end of each day, once they had fed and rested the potential was there for them to stray. During the first few days of a drove, the homing instinct was also strong in the beasts and they often had to be herded back. The watchman grew attuned to such nocturnal movements of the cattle. At other times they might be spooked by roaming deer, the moonlight, or the sheer weight of their numbers. In the early days, they were also at constant risk of cattle raiders from neighbouring glens.

Last night we were reading Haldane's book. He says: 'It almost seems that cattle raiding was, in the sixteenth and early seventeenth centuries, the chief occupation of the people of Scotland.'

During this time, King and Council sought every solution to the problem. They passed numerous acts of various types – keeping track of hides, requiring witnesses to check brand marks, and others – but stopping the cattle reivers was similar to ending any deeply engrained tradition. Reiving was a way of life, acceptable almost, which was why you stayed up all night to watch your herd.

*

Barnie was stung by a wasp this morning, as he wandered around the old, grassy station platform, Karrimat in hand. We dosed him with Piriton, and distracted him with tent pegs – clearly the toy of the moment. They make a great noise against tin mugs, and can be scattered around like pick-up-sticks to be picked up by Rob and Mum – the suckers.

Meanwhile, Ben looked on with a suspicious eye, and nipped the packs as we loaded them up for our second day on the road. Then he stepped on the doctor's toe, which was pretty ungrateful after Rob had worked so hard for his Pony Club D Test.

So it was that we set off, our happy peripatetic family, with only one bruised toe and one swollen face. None of this wiped the grins off our faces. We were off! Today is another adventure.

We covered the grand distance of two miles before stopping. This is the old Ballindalloch Station and we will leave the Speyside Way here. Barnie is asleep under a temporarily erected shelter, and Ben is tethered beside the road which leads to Cragganmore distillery. The distillery welcomes visitors and we both feel that Speyside requires a distillery tour; it is, after all, the reason many people come to this area in the first place.

Yet I am driven by the road and the good weather. We have only travelled ten miles in total, and stopping now feels as it might when you begin to paint a room but are forced to put down the brush after only a few strokes. We were just getting into the job.

Job? What job? Anticipation breeds anticipation, challenge breeds challenge; life on the road is as addictive as nicotine and I am champing at the bit to keep going and see what's around the next corner and the next. It is the one enemy of the road, this driving force; this boss who says go on and on. The coastal walk required the boss for successful completion, but now we both want to visit the distillery – and so it should be. We will stop here for the rest of the day and take whatever tomorrow offers us – rain or sun.

The farmer has just been past and told us we can put Ben in the field next to the station. He went off into the wide open with a buck and a fart, pleased to be free of both rein and chain. So we are going to put the tent up behind the station and spend the afternoon in the distillery.

*

The fiver spent visiting the Cragganmore distillery is money well spent. We are sated, happy people with puce faces and a better knowledge of the whisky process. I have also discovered the real meaning of what it is to be 'inside'; out of the wind, the sun, the glare. Nothing moves inside. A piece of grass doesn't sway, cobwebs don't break and everything stays where it's put. The stillness indoors is almost foreboding, like waiting for something to happen, and the sudden absence of elements brought fire to our cheeks and twinkles to the eyes. It is a grand feeling to come in from the cold and be warmed.

Of course, the whisky warmed us too. This was a good tumbler full, not the hint of liquid you are served in a pub which is normally about as much as you could squeeze from a feather. The fire spread further through our bodies, and even Barnie couldn't help partaking in the Water of Life as we were enveloped in the cloudy cumulus of malting steam.

Cragganmore is one of the six Classic Malts, which are whiskies selected to represent the best of the main whisky producing regions in Scotland, namely; Speyside, Islay, Skye, West Highland, Highland, Lowland. Yet the distillery is remarkably quiet and free from tourists on the 'whisky trail'. We were treated as VIPs – which was pretty good going for a motley pair of would-be drovers with their child of the road.

After the actual tour of the distillery, we retired to the exclusive Cragganmore Club where well-stuffed but well-used leather sofas absorbed us. Here, in the recreated sporting lodge drawing room, we were heated on the outside by the warmth of the open fire and from the inside by the product. We were given tea and shortbread, and the educational guidance of a whisky video.

It was from this room, with its Highland paintings and stuffed heads, that the founder of Cragganmore, John Smith, ran the distillery. It was founded in 1869, having the two advantages of its own spring on the nearby hill of Craggan More, and the proximity of the railway line. Cragganmore was the first distillery to lay on 'whisky specials' – long trains carrying thousands of gallons of whisky.

One corner of this mellow room is dedicated to Old Parr, who gave his name to a blended whisky produced at Cragganmore and described as having 'integrated smoky peat and spice elements on a mellow yet deep malt dominated palate'! Old Parr himself was a remarkable fellow by all accounts.

Thomas Parr was born in 1483 in America. He married for the first time at the age of eighty and had a son and a daughter. His wife died in 1595 and, ten years later, at the age of 122, Thomas married again.

In 1635, Thomas Howard, the second Earl of Arundel and Earl Marshal of England, heard of Thomas Parr and arranged for him to visit London where he was presented to King Charles I and painted by Rubens and van Dyck. He was 152 when he died. Cragganmore suggest that his secret to longevity was copious quantities of whisky!

We left the distillery with our minds once more on the drovers. Before whisky was legal, a lot of the amber nectar was transported around the country by the drovers. I can just see Ben with a couple of barrels lashed to his sides, though

I fear we would be no match in speed for the customs and excise men. Instead, we are brandishing one bottle to see us along the road. Whisky never tasted better than when you are enclosed by the darkening, russet hills from where the peaty water springs and begins its journey to become Water of Life – and to find its finale in the tin mug in your hand.

I am sitting on the old wooden bridge over the Spey, over which Ben clopped this morning without the hesitation of a hoof. The Spey flows relentlessly beneath the slats, and Tess is trying to shelter behind a rather thin girder. Barnie is asleep in the tent, and Rob is reading Haldane.

We have just had a delicious dinner of fried onions and garlic, mixed with a tin of aduki beans and a packet of cream of asparagus soup. Delicious – probably thanks to the setting and the hunger. Even Barnie wolfed it down, though I still had to pin him down and chase aduki beans several times around the camp site before they reached his mouth. I am glad there is no health visitor to witness such meal times.

When we were planning the trip, and the food we would eat, I suggested that we needed food simply to survive. Rob thought otherwise. He said that it takes up a good part of the day – lighting the stove, juggling pans, thinking up concoctions with the ingredients we have, trying to serve it all at a reasonable temperature. He was right. Food is a ritual of camping. It is around the stove that the camp revolves. All eyes are on the pots which bubble in anticipation, and hunger gears you for the feast; even Ben's horse nuts would probably be wolfed down with the help of a little cream of asparagus and garlic.

So what did the drovers eat?

In the absence of pasta, the drovers lived on oatmeal, onions, and blood. In Scott's *The Tale of Two Drovers* he adds to these ingredients; 'a ram's horn filled with whisky, which he [the drover] used regularly, but sparingly, every morning and night.' Sometimes, if they were lucky, they supplemented their diet with ewes' milk cheese and bannock.

The drovers carried their oatmeal in leather bags, and replenished their supplies whenever possible. On the whole, they mixed the oatmeal with cold water to make a type of porridge; other times they mixed it with the onions and blood to make black pudding.

Eighteenth-century Scottish farmers often bled their cattle during a hard winter, and blood procured in the spring or autumn was preserved to be eaten cold. It seems likely that the odd drover, short on food, might have bled a beast mid-drove.

We have been selective in recreating this part of the drove. We have the onions, the oats and oatcakes in abundance, and the contents of the rams horn. After that, we'll revert to pasta.

Daylight has vanished and the midges are finishing their supper. The wooded hills around are now featureless in black, and there is a big moon lying lazily on its side. The Speyside Way runs away into the night to the north and south, carrying in its darkness the imaginary whistles and pistons of ghostly steam engines. All is quiet and still. This is where I wanted to be; yet even here I cannot forget the cancer which brought on this trip.

I have a pain in my right side which is so annoyingly familiar, and which prevents me from forgetting about the cancer and the operation. As long as I have these pains, the worry brought on by cancer will plague me as determinedly as a Scottish midge. They say the pain is scar tissue, and that it will disappear... over time... Time is a random word plucked from infinity.

If I'm honest, this trip was an attempt to run away and forget that chapter of my life. Like sealing it with a large full stop. Perhaps I can't. Even here, now, with my mind on so many other things, the worries and pains surface like the unwelcome scars that they are; like oil on a pond. The scars are part of my album of memories which, on the whole, I enjoy flicking through. Many are bad, most are good, but I have to learn to look at the more recent painful memories, to stare them in the face and accept them for what they were.

Another Cup of Cold Coffee

Tuesday 10 September

Tess sleeps on the bottom half of Barnie's sleeping bag, but constantly squirms her way up until she squeezes Barnie out like the last remnants of toothpaste from a tube. I slept better last night in the knowledge that Ben was in a field, yet woke regularly to shovel Tess back down the tent and Barnie back into his sleeping bag.

Barnie wakes at 6.30 a.m., and demands our attention by clouting us with his beaker of ready-made powdered milk – hard. Then he makes an assault on Tess, who, now that Barnie's sleeping bag is vacant, makes herself at home within it. Mornings aren't particularly restful, nor are they romantic. We are thrown rudely into the day.

We left Ballindalloch at 9.20 a.m., which is pretty good going. Up and off doesn't happen. Already we are methodical in our feeding, packing and loading – as methodical as you can be with an apprentice toddler.

The two packs which hang either side of the wicker saddle are cycle panniers, adapted for the new role. They clip on to 'D' rings on the saddle and contain all the food, cutlery, books, torches and nappies (ideal as padding among the angular contents). The panniers have to be equally balanced otherwise they pull the saddle, and thus Barnie, one way or the other. Behind the saddle is a canvas crupper with buckles which we had made specially, and on to this we strap two custom made packs (roller bags with velcro). They also have to be equally balanced, and hold everything we do not need during the day; three sleeping bags, clothes and wash things. The tent and tarpaulin are strapped to the outside of these packs.

Strapping the packs on to Ben is a task in itself, especially if he is not tied up. This morning he had a good munch on the panniers while we struggled with the packs. There was suddenly an overpowering smell of fly spray and I looked down to see the white liquid pouring out from one pannier. Ben wrinkled up his nose in disgust. We had had a debate about whether to bring Ben's fly spray. If we didn't, the weather would be hot and the flies bad. If we did, the weather would do what it liked. So we brought it. But now... such a display of ingratitude on Ben's part! We binned the soggy remains; no self-respecting fly will come near us for sometime anyway.

The first mile was along the dead end road which leads down to Cragganmore, then we turned left on to the main A95. Near Bridge of Avon we made use of a large garage forecourt to get as far away from the road as possible. The attendant came running out as though expecting to serve us, but turned back into his shop and came out brandishing carrots and a Milky Bar. At first sight, nothing for Tess. Poor Tess. When we walked Britain's coast, she was the one fêted with biscuits and sweets. But now a carrot hovered within striking distance, and was gently snatched from the man's hand. Tess is adaptable. She loves carrots in the absence of anything remotely doggy.

Everyone chomped as we told the guy about the walk, and other garage and shop customers listened in. Then they produced money for the causes, wished us well and waved us off. If Rob and I had been walking alone along the road how different would have been our reception! Children, dogs, horses, they all break down barriers. They are an immediate link between people; an immediate topic of conversation. I don't believe that you could ever be lonely if you have one – if you have all three, your life will be full.

A little further on, after only half a mile of miserable main road, we turned off on to a brown road (as colour coded by the OS map). No sooner had we done so then a coach glided silently past, a row of faces pressed up to the windows in our direction. The coach stopped, and out poured the squashed faces. They were American and had cameras at the ready.

'Would you mind if we took your photo?' they asked, shivering in their thin yellow pullovers in the raw wind.

'It's a charity walk,' we said in reply.

They dug deep into their purses, and took plentiful photos. Funny to think we will go down through generations of American family albums; 'When I was in Scotland we saw...' 'When granny was in Scotland...' 'When your great-grandmother was in Scotland...' 'When your great-great-granny was in Scotland...' The photos will be dusty, faded and outdated, but there will be Barnie with Milky Bar dribbling down his chin and oozing through the gaps in his chin strap, and Ben grabbing hold of the backpack on my back, and Tess sitting shivering with her back to the camera.

The next person wasn't quite so friendly, and ordered us to put Tess on a lead.

'She's frightening the grouse,' he said, though I'm sure cars do more to frighten and kill grouse than well-fed Tess ever would. It was clear that he had simply got out of bed the wrong side, and we saw him again, a mile up the road, checking that we had done as told.

The road followed the River Avon to Glenlivet. Either side of us were thick trees which smothered the valley side and obliterated any view of the river. With the absence of much visual stimulation, Barnie's eyes were soon closing and his head nodding on Ben. We reverted to animal noises, and plenty of 'what's that? Ohh, look, there's a car!' in excited, intrepid voices. They kept him awake for a short time. We needed to stop for him to sleep, but could find no clearing suitable. All we needed was a grazing patch for Ben, a sheltered, safe place for Barnie to run around in, and a perfect view for us. It's not much to ask, really.

So we end up here, in a stony lay-by, facing the onslaught of the strong wind with an exhausted and miserable child on our hands. We try to put up the tent for Barnie to sleep in, but the pegs make no impression in the ground, so Rob holds it down with boulders and I'm grateful that we are in the hands of a Boy Scout.

Barnie is long since past his sell-by date. I try to feed him some warmed powdered food we have for just such emergencies, and in the process of opening the packet I cut my thumb. Blood goes everywhere and the food is now rippled with red. Not surprisingly, he won't eat the mush, and struggles against my grip as I try to calm him in the blowy tent. The sun shines through the flapping green nylon and makes me feel as though we are two peas in a pod waving on its pea branch. Barnie finally sleeps.

I crawl out of the tent (leaving another trail of blood) and Rob hands me a cup of coffee. The wind is sending waves across the surface of it, and the coffee is cold, again. The situation is improved by the opening of the chocolate eclairs. Good old Rob. He carries chocolate around as one might push a bicycle with a flat tyre. He never uses it – but, ahh, here we have the reason. I questioned the necessity of taking chocolate (added weight), but now it cheers me up no end. The flat-tyred bicycle comes in handy if faced with such life-threatening downhill emergencies.

Meanwhile, Tess is demonstrating that she is becoming accustomed to life on the road. As soon as we arrived here, she found herself a sunny, sheltered nook, and lay down to sleep. Ben, on the other hand, is flirting outrageously with a lady Clydesdale. The farmer here accosted us on the junction. He is the owner of three magnificent but redundant Clydesdales who trotted jauntily up and down the fence beside us. The farmer stood with his feet planted, ready for conversation. He spoke as so many do in these parts with a singalong accent crossed between Welsh and Yorkshire and punctuated by many 'ay ay's'. His news wasn't good.

'There'll be frost tonight, and they say there'll be snow on the hills, ay-ay.'

He suggested this spot to stop, and then, seeing Ben wrap himself several times around a spiky pine tree, he said we could turn him out in the field adjacent to the lady Clydesdale. At last, everyone is happy.

I am sitting on a log a little distance from Rob. The wind is whistling over the mouthpiece of the dictaphone so that it sounds as though I have a sock over my head. Another cup of coffee gone cold sits by my side.

Why are we here? If life was free from cut thumbs, screaming sons, billowing tents, cold coffee, rocky ground, would we be happy? When we get home people will ask whether we had fun, and I will say yes. I won't tell them about the misery because they will wonder why we carried on, voluntarily. But a trip like this is a microcosm of life; it has a beginning brimming with innocence and hope, a middle which matures with the highs and the lows, and an ending which must be faced whether with dread or an anticipation borne of achievement or uncertainty. 'Where do I go from here?' is something I thought as I stood on Tower Bridge at the end of the coastal walk in that moment of elation. I had dreaded the end, and the day when there was no longer a map in my hand. It feels good to be holding a map once more.

It has been our longest day yet – ten miles – and this is our first isolated camp spot. We are accompanied only by any ghosts which inhabit the ruined cottage of Craighead, now a rubble of rocks held together by a mortar of moss. The nearest house is a mile away. We can neither see nor hear anything of other lives. Instead, we are enclosed in an amphitheatre of hills topped with a green crown of forestry. The sun has dipped behind the crown to the west and a cold night threatens. The wind has eased, and darkness is descending as though a lid is being slowly lowered on to the bowl of the amphitheatre. All is quiet, except for the thunderous hooves of Ben as he tries to find some comfort in these alien surroundings.

From our lunch time spot, we followed a quiet road to Tomnavoulin. The road stayed high and the malty smell from the Glenlivet distillery hung in the valley. We passed the farm ominously named Gallowhill and looked down like voyeurs on the minuscule main road with its noisy tankers. The drovers remained on the River Avon, but we are finding our own route to avoid the road which now follows that river. At Tomnavoulin we turned off the road, on to the track which skirts the hill called Carn Daimh, and brought us here. Tomnavoulin has a distillery too, except that production stopped here five years ago. There is still several years worth of whisky maturing in barrels, and Tomnavoulin is still available in the shops. But the distillery is looking for a buyer – someone willing and rich. Rich enough to tide over the period of no production. I doubt that such a buyer will be found, unless it is the whisky magnate of United Distillers. It seems that the days of privately owned distillers have long since gone.

Our trip so far has been a little like a dot-to-dot of distillers, but I think Tomnavoulin was our last. Last distillery, first hill. Rob had to get behind Ben with his 'Wal' hat to encourage him up the hill to here, while I was pulling and heaving from the front. Despite the fact that it was 6 p.m. and long since past camp time and tea time, Barnie sat atop the stubborn Ben without a care in the world. We would get there, when the time suited Ben. No sooner, no later. And when we do, the supposedly exhausted horse sets off at a lumbering gallop across the field the farmer has allowed us to put him in. Contrary, that sums him up.

Rob is washing up in the burn below, and Barnie and Tess are sleeping. We are in for a cold night.

Tomintoul – the Highest Village in Scotland

Wednesday 11 September

It is an unfortunate town that has once been derided by the Queen of England. History remembers regal insults in a form similar to tabloid journalism and even now, well over a hundred years since Victoria visited Tomintoul, the village is preceded by her description of it as;

> The most tumble-down, poor looking place I ever saw – a long street with three inns, miserable dirty looking houses and people, and a sad look of wretchedness about it. Grant told me that it was the dirtiest, poorest village in the whole Highlands.

Tomintoul (pronounced 'Tumintowel'), was the creation of the fourth Duke of Gordon in 1776, who provided land for the village on either side of the military road. It is so clearly a planned village, with a road system which cuts the village into neat identical squares resembling cooking chocolate.

The long straight (military) main street runs through the middle, and off this is the central square of well-kept lawns, shady sycamore trees and tubs of flowers. When we visit it is neither miserable nor dirty nor wretched.

Overlooking the square on all sides are the low granite terraced houses, which so epitomise this area, facing inwards as though taking warmth from a central hearth. Such a square in Europe might accommodate outdoor tables and cafes; but here, 1,160 feet above sea level, you would expect a country market or fair where travellers sell their home-made wares and gypsies trade in horses. Ben certainly didn't look out of place.

One thing is certain; the drovers passed through here and, like us, gathered themselves before embarking on the harsher, more remote, more arduous terrain further south. Perhaps it was largely thanks to them, with their barrels of Speyside whisky or empty ram's horns, that Grant (who was the Parish minister of Tomintoul) said that the 'men, women and children [of Tomintoul] lived to sell and drink whisky.' Tomintoul doesn't have a distillery, but it does have the Whisky Castle – a testament to the people of whom Grant spoke?

The Whisky Castle is a small shop into which is squeezed every variety of whisky. It's presence in this small village, which boasts no more than a small handful of other shops (provisions are only available from an overgrown village store), illustrates the importance of whisky in Scotland and the Speyside region we have just left. To walk through Speyside without experiencing whisky would be like travelling through the Bordeaux region of France without mentioning wine, or driving through Cornwall without stopping for a cream tea.*

Tomintoul is a milestone for us. It is our fourth day on the road, and we have reached our first cache of goodies. Part of the planning of the trip was to pack up parcels of nappies, wipes, fuel, horse food, dog food, dried milk, various dried foods unlikely to be found in such places as Tomintoul – and the odd treat. We dropped these at various places on our way up here – tourist information centres, village shops, pubs or estate factors (estate managers). Picking up and opening the big black bag today was like Christmas.

Today started cold, and we ate porridge wearing every article of clothing. Barnie finds movement hard in all his layers, and when he topples over he is like a tortoise cast on its back. Puce-faced and blue-handed, he waves his limbs in the air and wails to be righted. The sun then appeared over the hill. Being warmed and dried by the gradual heat of the sun as it climbs up through the sky is one of life's most pleasurable experiences. It is quite unlike being warmed by artificial heat which is so quick and sudden that the body is involuntarily forced to adjust.

The other thing which warms us up is packing up and saddling Ben – all of which is hard with a thumb enclosed in a bandage of disproportionate size. Rob has Barnie on his back when we saddle up. I am taking no chances, ever since the day at home when I looked down to see him crawling

---

*Scotland produces a staggering 2,500 types of whisky - (not bad for apopulation of around 5.1m). In total, there are around 97 distilleries. Go anywhere in the world, and Scotland is synonymous with whisky; walk Speyside, and it appears at every turn.

between the skyscraper legs of Ben as he might crawl among climbing frame legs.

We set off uphill, breaking through the crown of woodland which enclosed us last night. Ben found the woodland spooky, seeing shadows and ghouls in every twist of a branch. I try to relax when he is on his toes, knowing that apprehension flows through the leading rope to him, but it is sometimes hard when I think of the precious cargo he carries.

When we emerged from the wood, the scene ahead held my attention as though the theatre curtains had opened to reveal a staggering set. The heather moorland dropped gently away in front of us towards slopes occasionally painted in the rich green of forestry. Behind these, the hills of the Grampians and Eastern Cairngorms held up their peaks in salute.

It crossed my mind then how different it is to be without the sea constantly on our right; that big watery blue which soothes the dry eye. Here, every step produces the scene from a slightly different angle, like a picture book flipped through at speed to produce a 360 degree flowing picture, a film with the theme of green.

We walked down through the heather with springs in our strides. Tess raced around and around in the heather, rolling and throwing herself down with sheer delight. Ben, on the other hand, behaved as Tess once did, and tittuped through the heather as though wearing stilettos, worrying about what might emerge from its tangled depths.

As the path became narrower, and large boulders lurked beneath the heather, I was guiding Ben with every step. My eyes were Ben's eyes. Ahead of us, Rob sung the path into existence:

'And the wild mountain thyme
Blooms across the purple heather
Will ye go, lassie, go.
And we'll all go together
To pick wild mountain thyme
All among the purple heather
Will ye go, lassie go...
Lassie go.'

At the edge of this moorland set we came to a layer of pines. They seemed impenetrable, but there was a passable corridor, zigzagged with drainage ditches. We put Barnie on Rob's back and led Ben over the ditches. After this, it was a stretch of marshy grass and a series of burns to negotiate. Ben was soon leaping the burns, undeterred by the packs slapping against his sides. I saw purpose in Ben's eyes.

Back at home, I long-rein Ben in his driving harness. As yet we have no cart, so this ensures that Ben doesn't forget what it is like to be blinkered and driven. I carry Barnie on my back, and Tess trots alongside, and in this fashion we follow both country lanes and housing estate avenues. Once we took a short cut across the corner of a ploughed field. Ben bent his head down and put all his concentration into the task. Walking behind him, through the heavy clods of earth which stuck to each hoof and step, and watching his big brown bottom taking the strain, I felt for a brief moment what it was like to work the land with horses. It didn't seem necessary to have a plough to experience the feeling of belonging and oneness. And when I got home that day, I watched Ben once he was turned out in the field. He went for a drink, had a good roll, then he munched on his hay with an aura of fulfilment encircling him. He seemed so peaceful. How much better that drink or delicious dinner tastes at the end of a day of fulfilment. Everyone needs such purpose, belonging and sense of achievement. I could see it today in Ben's eyes. There are times when he is apprehensive, times when he is reluctant, and times when he exasperates – yet he rises to his purpose and role.

We popped out on to the lane which led us here, to Tomintoul. The lane follows the con tours of a steep sided valley through patches of birch woodland clinging on to old sheep pasture. Away above the valley, buzzards circled, gliding on thermals and calling their territory, their shadows causing tiny mammals to bolt for cover. What graceful, effortless predators they are. Barnie was fascinated with them and clearly confused them with aeroplanes.

It was late lunch time when we arrived in Tomintoul. No sooner had we clopped into the High Street then the population, young and old, batty and sane, flocked around Ben like flies to a sweaty horse. The most insistent were the schoolchildren on lunch break. They looked sombre in black uniforms and ate chips from paper cones. They wanted to pat Ben and Tess, but were reluctant to part with any chips. In the end I had to prompt them. Meanwhile, Rob was trying to find a field for Ben and a B&B for us.

'The lady at the trekking centre will have a field,' everyone said.

So we dragged the tired Ben off there. The place was deserted except for fields of interested horses, so we dragged him back. Uphill and away from mates is the worst scenario for an exhausted Ben, and so Rob resorted to the hat treatment, then the physically-push-Ben-treatment. We worked in silence. It wasn't just Ben who was tired and thirsty; our tanks were also running low. We considered stopping in the square and grazing Ben on the neat grass, but eventually we would have had to move, and packing up an extra time was not something we relished.

We were accompanied throughout this ordeal by a batty lady who came ever closer to Ben before repeatedly claiming that she was 'terrified of horses', then declaring 'ohh what a shame' for no apparent reason. While Barnie watched the whole thing as though it was a pantomime entirely for his benefit, my fuses were getting shorter and shorter. A well aimed Clydesdale foot would have solved the problem.

In reply, Ben ground his teeth as he does when he's thirsty, and stamped his feet as he does when he's tired. But never in the right direction.

'There's the common field at the end of town,' some kind person eventually confessed. 'It's where the Tomintoul Games are held. You can put him there.'

And so Ben is grazing this sacred land, and we are ensconced in a B&B. I have removed my T-shirt for the first time since Sunday, and Barnie has been in the shower with me. We are squeaky clean and ready to hit the night spots of Tomintoul.

Bringing Up Barnie

Barnie's second home in his first few weeks was the post office. Here, wedged into his car seat, he sat among a forest of pasty Scottish legs bared by the appearance of the rare Scottish sun. Every now and then a face loomed down into his world, cooed, and shrank away again. Barnie blew bubbles and gazed indifferently at the legs. It can't have been a pretty introduction to his species.

Barnie's birth coincided with the publication of my first book. So, while he studied varicose veins, I battled with mountains of parcelled books. Like all twins, this joint birth wasn't a conscious decision but it was one I had to live with. Every day I went to the post office, Barnie dangled from one arm, and books from the other. Not so long ago they had both been inside me, one in my head and the other in my womb. Now I carried them around as baggage. And what baggage!

Friends and family can cushion the fall into motherhood with warnings and help, but it is still a shocking realisation that things will never be the same again. Spontaneity disappears like an extinguished candle. Puff and gone. In *its place has to be some sort of planning, some orderliness, to get through the days. Added to this is the disappearance of selfishness.*

Suddenly I realised what all these other mothers had been up to all these years. I used to be one of those who stood at the supermarket checkout wondering why mothers took so long; and listened disbelievingly to mothers complaining about such (previously) inconsequential things as inadequate supermarket trolleys. Why aren't there trolleys designed for newborn babies? Aren't new mothers supposed to eat? The only thing on offer was a wide steamroller-of-a-trolley with a child seat manufactured of concrete plastic, which looked about as comfortable as a station bench – guaranteed to have your child howling with discomfort. My solution was to use the disabled trolley – a flat platform which accommodates the car seat easily, but little else.

At ten days old, Barnie accompanied me to the supermarket to shop for the book launch party; Pimms, lemonade, nibbles, wine, beer, fruit for the Pimms. The limited space around Barnie is full after the fruit section. Before long I have taken the fruit from their bags and wedged them around Barnie so that he looks like an exotic cocktail. All he needs is a speared cherry in his teeth and a wedge of lemon on each ear. At least now there is a little room for the booze. A Guinness can falls and punctures, spraying a huffy, presumably childless female. 'Just you wait,' I mutter, as so many others probably said to me. I balance more tins and more bottles. What do people think of me? Driven to the bottle already, no doubt. Big Time Boozing Mother. Supermarkets have never been the same.

Barnie handled the book launch party with the same nonchalance he had handled life until this time. It was just the way it was. Unfortunately this was the last time I saw him so relaxed for some time.

Colic in babies is what car mechanics are to the average person – an enigma. The difference with cars is that you can call the AA and all will be OK. 'To our members, we're the fourth emergency service.' Well, there should be a fifth to deal with colicky babies. Almost overnight Barnie was transformed from a placid baby to a wailing engine. Like the little wren, I would look at Barnie and wonder 'how can such a small thing make a noise of such volume?'

One short month of colic; yet I feared it would last forever. As time went slowly on, I convinced myself that I had a miserable child on my hands; that I had somehow brought this on. Perhaps an unhappy pregnancy meant an unhappy baby? Perhaps the father had some hidden streak of sheer misery which I had never witnessed? My days were spent holding Barnie, rocking him, trying everything – and then despairing. When he slept, I parcelled books. Books and babies are not a good combination; just as I crawled into my bed, he woke up and the crying resumed. Thank goodness for the maroon pram and the front sling, but there is only so much walking even I can do. Besides, I was trying to get Barnie into some sort of 'routine' – that dreaded word passed down from our Victorian ancestors.

'If Barnie sleeps in your bed it'll be the end! He'll never want to sleep on his own!' I am warned (picturing a spotty adolescent who still insists on sleeping with his mother).

Never mind that temporarily having Barnie in bed makes my life so much easier.

Besides, is a four week old child capable of such manipulation? 'If you hold Barnie all the time he'll never learn independence! Let him cry,' people advise. Yet whenever I put him down he wails and I think I am failing. Oh Lordy Be... Motherhood – an onslaught of conflicting advice.

My greatest support was Barnie's adopted Granny, Madge, who lived in the other end of our semi-detached farm cottages and provided the experience and love that any granny could. She was my saviour, and there were many others, but I was the mother and evenings alone were the worst. Barnie reached a crescendo at 9 p.m. before eventually crashing out at about 10 p.m., by which time I was like a used and crumpled tissue – soggy with Barnie's tears, creased with exhaustion, and torn around the edges.

One night, after Barnie had eventually fallen asleep, I went to the cupboard to find something to eat. It was always a question of whether hunger overcame tiredness, and on this occasion it did. I opened the cupboard and out flew a beautiful, soft, sleepy moth – almost the sole inhabitant of the larder. A few skinny strands of pasta looked as if even they had lost weight, and several packets of pulses shook their heads and declared 'uh uh, need planning'. The moth flew off and out of the kitchen door and I was sorely tempted to follow. Oh to be winged and free! Oh to be childless again, and eat, sleep, live and party. I sat down and cried lonely tears on more than this one occasion. Perhaps my sister, my family and some friends had been right, and

*this whole motherhood lark was just too hard on your own.
I was glad they weren't here to see me.*

*The next day I took Barnie to the Health Centre. The
health visitor checked his progress. He was stacking on the
weight, literally ounces per day – were these growing pains
he was experiencing? She then asked me if I was enjoying
him. I stared at her. Enjoying him? Was she serious? The
words 'colic' and 'enjoy' can never ever conceivably be
used in conjunction with one another; or was I missing
something? Incredulity must have passed over my face, then
guilt.*

*Apart from Madge and friends, there were two things
which kept me going. The first was Ben. He arrived mid-
colic, when Barnie was a month old, and in times of despair
I fled the cottage to find comfort in his sanity. I climbed
on to his broad, warm, brown back and let him graze the
grass outside the cottage. His karma was good; unflustered,
non-judgemental, the middle way. Tess was the same, except
that it was hard to find her. The only time she helped was to
introduce me to the term baby-sit – you find the baby then sit
on it. This usually resulted in Barnie emitting a fart of grand
proportions, illustrating this to be a far more efficient way of
winding your baby than any back slapping. But otherwise
Tess spent most of this month curled up in the folds of a
duvet in the furthest corner of the cottage. Lucky, wise dog.*

*The second thing was the smile. Rare though it was, it
appeared at just over four weeks, like a weak spring sun
which has yet to gain strength and energy. It showed me
that somewhere, within that little, wracked and spotty body,
was a moth just waiting to emerge.*

One evening a friend phoned just as things were at their worst, and fifteen minutes later she arrived on our doorstep. She marched straight into the kitchen, held her hands up in horror at the bomb site before her, and began cleaning up. 'If your world's tidy and in order you'll feel so much better,' she declared. With that done, she took Barnie from me and put a large joint into my hands. It was hardly a fair swap, a crying baby for fleeing reality.

We sat outside in the evening June sun. The swallows did their thing through the large barns opposite the cottage, swooping and swerving and dipping and diving, catching their mid-flight meals. Do young swallows get colic? Ben hung his head over the gate, dozing. His bottom lip wobbled in undiluted relaxation and the same feeling swept through my body and then through Barnie's. The world was the right way up again, no longer turned on its head and gravity-less. The next time I saw my friendly doctor I suggested he prescribed a little marijuana to flustered mothers in charge of colicky babies.

But I was lucky. I lived in a fantastic cottage with open space all around in which to escape. I thought constantly of mothers living in high-rise blocks, in crime ridden, violent inner city areas. How on earth do they cope? And what if I already had other children, demanding toddlers or bored six year olds? Violence to children is deplorable and unacceptable in any situation; but now I could see, just a little more clearly, its causes.

The colic disappeared almost overnight when Barnie was six weeks old. The crying hours became a memory. 'Enjoy' became a word I understood. It was August and the sun shone, as I walked the lanes and tracks with Ben, Barnie and Tess, dreaming and talking in my one-sided monologue, asking questions and giving myself the answers I most wanted to hear – the perfect dialogue. At the time of our six-week post-natal check up, I changed doctors. The female doctor admired my flat stomach and said 'it seems you are designed for having babies.' I remembered those words with pride, unaware of the fall to come. They would be cruel words in retrospect.

She then took a smear, something I hadn't had for four years. It wasn't that I was consciously avoiding them, it was just that I hadn't been registered with a doctor for some time. I wouldn't have been registered with one now if I hadn't got pregnant and, as any woman knows, a smear is not something you relish. I was lucky that this Health Centre was on the ball and that my doctor was insistent. How easy it would have otherwise been to walk out of that door having avoided this undignified process...

A couple of weeks later, I bundled Barnie on to the train to London, then the sleeper to Penzance, then the ferry to the Isles of Scilly. Apart from several weekends away to the Highlands, this was his first taste of travel. We lay in our sleeper cabin and the station lights flashed through the night like dreams through the subconscious. Brakes squealed and whistles blew, and disembarking passengers spoke in hushed holiday voices. I was awake at first light, too excited about our forthcoming holiday with all three of my sisters, their six children and brave Grandpa. Cornwall was slowly unveiled in the twilight, green and hilly with narrow, muddy lanes and sleek dairy cows busy producing clotted cream.

Out in the corridor, I pulled down the window and let the early morning blow in; the smell of the sea, salty lobster pots and fishy crates. Flowering gorse hung heavy on the air and the smells whizzed past, taking me back to childhood holidays and the coastal walk. Barnie slept on. In fact, he had fallen asleep in his pram in London and never stirred until I had to wake him in Penzance. He was proving to be a good traveller.

After two weeks of sunshine and beaches on the car-less island of Tresco, we repeated the journey home. I felt, now, I could take my son anywhere; the world was ours to explore. A pile of mail and book orders waited at home. Among it was a letter saying that abnormal cells had been found from my smear. I would have to attend a colposcopy clinic to have them removed. No cause for alarm, no need to panic; many women undergo this every day, I was assured.

My ex-doctor, now friend, also reassured me. I saw a good deal of Rob, though I found it hard to see him as anything other than a doctor – one of 'them'. But little by little we got to know each other through trips to the Highlands. We walked and talked, and talked and walked, visiting Iona, Skye, Mull and many places in between.

I rarely thought of the forthcoming colposcopy. I had had no previous experience of ill health, and therefore no foundation stone on which to build a tower of fear. This was just a blip in the continuum. The appointment came and went. I left the hospital minus a few abnormal cells and thought that was that. Except it wasn't.

Two days later, on a Friday afternoon, just as The Archers was ending and Barnie was lying on the floor waggling his *legs in time to the theme tune, the doctor appeared on my doorstep.*

She was so out of context that I struggled to realise who she was. When I did, I had no time to wonder at what she was doing here before her words hit me; 'I'm sorry, Spud. There's no easy way to say this. You've got cervical cancer.'

In the Hands of Estate Factors

Thursday 12 September

Sleep is such an issue with babies; why is it that they find it so hard to fall asleep? Is it just that life is too exciting to miss out on anything? Or do they miss the sleep-inducing movement of being in the womb? Barnie has no problem falling asleep on Ben, or on Rob's back, but in a sleeping bag on the floor he battles valiantly to keep his eyes open.

It feels as though I spent most of yesterday putting Barnie to sleep. Once when he woke early in the morning, once at his midday sleep, and again when we returned from our Tomintoul night life. I long for a cot to plonk him in. When he woke at 6 a.m. this morning I wondered if we would be defeated. He is asleep now, lying on cushions on the floor of the B&B lounge. The colour drains from his face when he sleeps and he looks expressionless yet content. Is he storing up these experiences for use later? His innocence has won me over. I have decided that he will get another chance.

Meanwhile, I am doing a spot of needlework. For me, needlework at school was about as successful as joining the choir. I was told there was no hope after repeatedly sewing whatever it was to my skirt and having to be rescued. But now the canvas crupper needs attention. The packs have been swinging too low and annoying Ben's back legs as he walks. Rather hopefully, we feel this might be aggravating his snail's pace and anything which may mean a little less pulling and pushing is worth trying.

Meanwhile, Rob is gathering our washing together and repacking the bags. It is a scene of drovers' domesticity. From Tomintoul, the River Avon offers an obvious route south through the Grampians. It starts its passage from Loch Avon, high up in the Cairngorms, and is an amalgamation of numerous peaty burns with unpronounceable Gaelic names. Avon itself is pronounced 'Arn', proclaiming its identity from that river on which Shakespeare's home town sits.

It is a beautiful river, hustling its way over boulders and squeezed between the heather hills on either side. Every now and then it is swelled by smaller burns with such wonderful names as Muckle Fergie Burn and its sister, Burn of Little Fergie. But flowing water doesn't have the same place here as it does in the Western Highlands, where water is squeezed from every rock and sprig of heather. Here, its passage is more gentle without the rugged rocky escarpments, craggy con tours and scrubby, bushy gullies.

The hills of the Grampians are rounded shingly mounds, like air-filled Exmoor, pumped up, inflated, to produce hills of importance. They appear smooth and kind, like the rounded bellies of pregnant moorland. It is a landscape which allows the eye to roam freely, uninterrupted by the rough features which make the Western Highlands what they are. Above all, the Grampians give you a tremendous feeling of space. Huge, massive, air-filled space.

I enjoyed following the River Avon. Apart from anything, this was the exact route taken by the drovers, to whom the rivers were the transport network with their flat valleys and natural barriers from outside raiders and elements. We were expecting to follow a gravel track along the riverside this afternoon, but this has been upgraded to a tarmac road. A tarmac road to nowhere; except Inchrory Lodge, an enormous shooting lodge hugged tightly within the grip of the hills where the River Avon accepts Builg Burn.

Inchrory Lodge is seven miles from the nearest habitation and has been deserted for many years. But now it has been purchased by an Arab with money aplenty. He is renovating the lodge beautifully – the only trouble is, he knows his punters will want all mod cons. He also knows they will want entertainment laid on when they aren't out shooting animals. So he is laying pipes and poles, and building leisure facilities, and a tennis court. At the start of the track-turned-road which we followed through the glen we saw a sign saying 'Tennis Courts'. We looked at each other.

'Tennis courts? Up here?'

It was like some sort of April Fool hoax. Back at home, people don't take guns to the tennis court. Are we incapable of doing one thing and one thing only? The signs continued intermittently down the glen. Stuck to trees like coloured stains on a black and white photo, they needed to be erased from the harmonious landscape. Then came the phone and telegraph poles. It is strange, but the telegraph poles you see as part of your world every day are acceptable and accepted. But these ones grate with their intrusion. The reason people will come here is to enjoy the unspoilt nature of such country, yet why haven't they buried the lines? Money probably. And why haven't they used the same poles for power and telephone instead of erecting two lines? There probably is some reason, but this is how so many other glens started their transition from peaceful haven to valley of communication.

Despite all the work at Inchrory, the road was quiet. It only became busy at knock-off time when the boys raced back along the road to Tomintoul, clearly thirsty, and little expecting to find anyone else on their road; let alone a horse, a child jockey, a rabbit-frenzied dog, a bearded doctor with a Wal hat and skin tight Ronhills, and a...

To begin with, the glen was quite wooded. But as the heathery bellies increased in size they began to pinch the river and force out the vegetation. We covered four miles before being drawn by the ample, beautiful camping spots on the grassy river banks. Large enough areas to tether Ben, fresh water, flat land for the tent, shelter. Each spot looked more tempting, more peaceful. Just as we were sizing one up, a Land Rover came into sight and pulled up alongside us. A man's face filled the open window, looking us up and down and making clear that he thought little of what he saw. 'Where are you off to?'

Rob, ever the tactful, polite, law-abiding citizen was made to look as though he had just robbed a bank by this officious factor. He explained what we were doing, falteringly, and added that we were looking for a camping spot.

'You can't camp here,' came the reply. 'We're stalking tomorrow. You'll have to get past Inchrory Lodge itself. It's only another six miles.'

Six miles is the whirl of a hub cap in a land rover, but it was 4.30 p.m. and we had a soon-to-be hungry child on a horse. I know little about stags or stalking, but I know they use garrons* and, anyway, the glen was alive with the sound of workmen's labours. A small family camped by the side of the river would surely disturb the deer less than that?

The man drove off with a roar of his vehicle and a spray of gravel. Rob let out an uncharacteristic expletive, and began his encourage-Ben-on-with-his-Wal-hat-routine. Tess, unperturbed by this news, was busy culling 'myxi' rabbits.

A little further on another Land Rover pulled up. We braced ourselves for an onslaught, but the man could not have been more charming. We chatted for a while, watched by a glassy eyed stag which lolled in the back of the Land Rover. I wondered whether Ben would be perturbed by the presence and smell of deer in these hills. We have seen plenty eyeing us up from their hill tops like the guardians of the land they are, but so far Ben seems ignorant of their presence.

We reached this spot past Inchrory at about 6.30 p.m. Barnie was still remarkably content and is delighted with the amateur rock face we are camped near. He loves rock climbing, small scale, and it kept him amused while we

*Highland ponies used for bringing the shot stags down from the hills.

102

unpacked, tethered Ben, put up the tent, and got food on the go. Peeping through some trees, half a mile north from here, is the white mass of still-empty Inchrory Lodge.

Slowly, gradually, the sun dropped away and the resulting shadow slid gracefully across the glen floor and up the other side until it hit the horizon and made silhouettes of the hills. Unseen deer roam freely over their terrain, and only the midges accompany us. Ben is intent on his grazing. He has had his handful of nuts – a small token of appreciation really for carrying our mountains of stuff. He drags his ghostly chain and seems quite settled for now, but tonight will be his biggest test yet; the wide open spaces, the isolation and possibility of deer visitations.

Barnie has now gone to bed, accompanied by his well-travelled and very grubby penguin which receives more attention from Tess than from Barnie. He is also accompanied by Tess, who craves the warmth of the tent but is always worried that she is missing out on something. We zip her into the tent with Barnie, but very soon she is scratching to come out again. In, out, in, out she goes. The sound of zips must accompany Barnie on his dreams. Outside, by the light of a candle, Rob and I revel in our situation. This is where I longed to be for so long. No one knows exactly where we are; and where we are is at the whim of the elements. It is impossible not to sense our insignificance out here, and our mortality.

Cancer has made me doubly aware of my mortality. Three years ago I was stung by a bee and had a major reaction. I had been stung numerous times before, but anaphylactic shock can develop at any time. The doctor saved my life with intravenous adrenaline and I now have to carry adrenaline at all times. If a bee stings me, I have no more than half an hour to live unless injecting myself immediately. It is weird to watch little bees with big stings buzzing around in the summer, and it is weird to have had my life saved twice by doctors. The bee escapade undoubtedly heightens the cancer fears; if one doesn't get me, will the other?! I know we all have to go sometime, but the expression 'being run over by a bus' has changed in real terms to become 'being stung by a bee.'

This evening, as Barnie was practising his walking and I was helping him negotiate the obstacles of heather and dip, he repeatedly reached out for my hand when he needed it, when the going got tough. I thought then that I hope I will always be there for him, as he grows up and when he is grown up, so that he can take my hand when the going gets tough. I know I still reach out for my father's hand.

My fear of dying and leaving Barnie has been my greatest fear. If I had been childless and diagnosed with cancer, that would have been bad enough; or if I knew Barnie's father would be there to take care of him and love him doubly, that would have been enough too. But the fear of him being left alone in this mad world, that is where the fear sometimes flows like ice in my blood. How many times have I looked at him and thought; 'what would happen to you?' Then the thought is too chilling and painful and I push it aside. Such fear is so frighteningly physical and it doesn't help to tell people because they just say 'yes, but the cancer won't come back,' even if they have their own fear that it will. Besides, it is frightening to talk of such things. I am lucky that the cancer was discovered early. It was removed with my womb before any real spread had occurred and I am cured now. But there is a chance that it might come back and having been hit once it is hard not to worry. No one can be philosophical all the time.

Dear Barnie. Will I love him to death? I wondered today, when the officious factor told us where to go, about my decision to bring him out here. It is a big thing for a little lad so far from home. What if things go wrong?

Up a Glen Without a Horse

Friday 13 September

An ominous quiet sat in the still glen this morning, like the silence of snow or a house in a power cut when all electric appliances have ceased their humm. I lay in my sleeping bag hoping that Ben was out there, but knowing with a mother's instinct that he wasn't. Sure enough, I poked my head out of the tent and scanned a horse-less scene, then checked again as though I might have missed Ben's handsome hulk the first time. It was pointless. Ben was hardly likely to be momentarily hidden behind a tussock of grass or lying under a rock like a sun-shy insect. Only the white eye of Inchrory blinked back at me through the morning light.

I relayed the bad news to Rob, and threw on my clothes, shaking. Somewhere out there was a horse dragging fifteen foot of metal links. Was he snagged on a tree? Had he then panicked and fallen down the bank into the river, hanging by his chain? Had he tried to cross the weak bridge we had avoided over the Avon yesterday? Or had he gone right back to Tomintoul? In which case we were stuck. Quite literally, up a glen without a horse. Imagination is a curse of a thing at such times. In the back of my mind I knew that we had passed a couple of garrons just before Inchrory. Ben had been reluctant to leave them, and had probably gone back there to tell them how severely cheesed off he was with the situation. I set off, headcollar and Polos in hand, following the drag mark of the chain which resembled the track of an indecisive snake.

I called as I walked, tentatively, as though my voice might disturb the quiet and bring on some sort of reproach. I thought of Black Beauty and all the other fabled, loyal horses. Would Ben hear my voice and come galloping gallantly over the rise? Not a chance. Then I saw his white blaze look up and his ears prick. Sure enough, there he was colluding with the two garrons. It might have been wishful thinking or cupboard love or both, but he appeared quite pleased to see me and came back to camp quietly. While we de-camped, he lay down in the sunshine to sleep off the exhausting affects of his foray – the prodigal horse returned.

The roof of the tent had acted as a rain measuring device during the night, and Rob had had to dress Barnie while dodging the ensuing falls. But the sun soon dried us out, and finally we were off again. As we stood there, Ben loaded, Barnie boarded, and said goodbye to another flattened campsite, Rob and I looked at each other and smiled. It is the same every day; the close companionship brought on by life on the road; by routine, by the highs and lows and overcoming both. Rob and I moved into a cottage together two weeks before this trip. Both the cottage and our relationship were fairly chaotic when we left last week. It isn't easy to amalgamate two houses, two lives and a combined total of sixty years of diverse experience into one place. Now the turmoil of moving in together has been forgotten as we rediscover life's priorities.

Our lives are so different at home – him a busy doctor, me a mother and dilettante. Here, now, we are on common ground and working towards the same goal, and it feels good. Expeditions can either make or break friendships or relationships.

We are camped for lunch near the ruins of Loch Builg Lodge, though 'Lodge' is a rather grand word for the pile of rubble inhabited only by a deranged mouse with no fear and a sticking up tail. It is quite extraordinary, darting from stone to stone with its stilted stagger, oblivious of our presence and probably the fact that it is a mouse. *The Mouse of Loch Builg* sounds like a good name for a children's story.

Barnie the droving bairn is asleep on a Karrimat under the waterproofs. Tess the drovers' dog is lying on the other end of the Karrimat under a fleece, keeping one eye on the manic mouse and the other on the strewn contents of the panniers – lunch of oatcakes, Primula, dried apricots. Wal is studying the map. There appears to be no evidence of crofting here. There are no lazy-beds, and little grazed, sheep-rich pasture encircling the two old buildings. There is just a small area of cropped grass littered with small yellow saffron flowers, and then the blanket of heather begins, rolled out towards the edge of Loch Builg and up into the hills. Loch Builg itself is a beautiful high loch of milky, almost phosphorescent appearance.

This was, however, almost definitely a 'stance' for the drovers (a place where they stopped with their beasts for the night). We are still treading in their exact footsteps, along the steep sided Glen Builg and past Loch Builg to here. This flat land with its fresh water supply would have been an ideal stance, and the Lodge was probably the scene of many a drovers' yarn. Stances were an essential part of the drove. The beasts usually covered ten to twelve miles per day, and their ability to cover these distances day after day, week after week, depended on adequate rest, food and water at night. The topsman went ahead of the beasts to organise these stances, but as time went on and the legal droving trade was established, recognised stances were used time and again.

The beasts were fenced in only by the glen walls, and the grazing was normally free of charge. In fact, in some areas the droves were welcome because the passage and pasturage of the cattle meant valuable manuring. To this day, some of the stances remain greener and lusher thanks to the thousands of cattle who manured them.

Ben added his contribution to manuring the stance at lunch time and when we packed him up again he leapt in the air and squealed like a thoroughbred colt. I think his days as a Highland packhorse are numbered, and future trips will stick to lowland tracks and neat field systems befitting an agoraphobic horse. At the moment he is like an overtired child.

Because of Ben's antics, Rob carried Barnie all afternoon. We had been planning to camp somewhere between Loch Builg and Invercauld but a combination of Ben's behaviour and the cold wind, which brewed up a bank of ominous cloud, made us rethink. The other option was to continue on to Invercauld on the River Dee, where the factor had previously said we could put Ben in a field. We set off from Loch Builg without quite knowing where we would get to, and turned south west to follow the River Gairn where lazy-beds and rubbles of stone indicated a once thriving glen and gave credence to our journey. At one time the glen would have been home to mothers and bairns with their crofting fathers and uncles, and the whinny of a Highland pony might have given Ben security. How sad it is that these deserted communities have vanished, and how wicked was the way they were 'cleared' to make way for sheep.

We branched away from the river and began to scale Culardoch. We walked in silence, absorbed by the enormity of the scenery, and every step brought better and better views; across the Gairn to the nipple-like tors of Ben Avon smothered in ash grey shingle which merged with the heather at a lower level. Below us, the River Gairn followed the glen like a white ribbon through the grey-green country. Then, at the top, on the shoulder of the 900-metre Culardoch, we caught our first sight of the country to come; the Dee valley and Lochnagar. A little later we saw Mount Keen for the first time.

Every so often we stopped and looked back to the vast, spacious country behind slipping silently out of view, turning the page on another stretch of country. Then it was gone and we were heading downhill to the next valley; and the lower we got, the faster the clouds converged on the land behind us like encroaching waves on an incoming tide.

The track was still good, and we made good speed. But even when the hills behind had been entirely obliterated by the weather, and Rob voiced his concerns, there were no clearings in which to tether Ben and camp. Our decision to continue to Invercauld was made. The rain just stayed off until we had passed through an area of old Caledonian forest, then scuttled through some less exciting imported pines, and hit the tracks of Invercauld. Relief and excitement at reaching this new valley was mingled with concern and a strong desire to stop, put up camp, and get warm. We kept Barnie going with in-flight meals of a last squidgy Tomintoul banana and, yup, more oatcakes.

Evening brought with it rain and a cold wind, but we are happy here muffled up to our noses and sitting on chairs at a candlelit table in a garage, feeling for all the world as though we are in the Ritz. Simon the factor is brilliant, and arriving in this foreign land at the late hour would have been miserable if it wasn't for him.

His four daughters helped him produce this table and chairs and even an old pushchair for Barnie, who was wedged tightly into it by all his layers at tea time. At least it kept him still for a while. Meanwhile, Ben is happy in the companionship of a Shetland and a garron.

We have covered twelve and a half miles today. Inchrory feels like a distant land. Barnie is asleep now, zipped snugly into his thermal all-in-one (cosily called a 'Chuckroast'). Tess is babysitting him in the tent while we celebrate Invercauld and achievement in our garage palace.

The Big 'C'

'I'm sorry Spud. There's no easy way to say this. You've got cervical cancer. You'll need a hysterectomy.'

My initial thought was 'Poor doctor. What a horrible job it must be to deliver bad news to people!' Then, like a temporarily dazed animal, I came to and realised what she had said. Or tried to.

How quickly one's life can be turned upside down. A few minutes ago I was listening to the late John Archer rant on about his pigs and Eddie Grundy getting up to more mischief. Ten minutes ago I had been talking to my cousin in West Linton, talking mother talk and cousin talk. Then I had worried about Barnie's nappy rash, or what I should wear to the wedding tomorrow, or whether Ben needed new shoes just yet. Everyday stuff on an everyday Friday. Now a curtain had come down separating that life from this. The world had been turned upside down and shaken hard. Nothing was as it should be.

Barnie was lying on the floor smiling broadly at life and the doctor. I picked him up instinctively, and the fateful road which had led to this moment flashed through my mind as I *cuddled the only child I would have. There would be plenty of denial to overcome before really accepting this situation – but my decision of less than a year ago could never have been otherwise. What if…?*

Then I didn't know what to do or say. I was soon to realise that being diagnosed with cancer throws you into a scene for which there are no lines, a play with no script. Instead, your life is swept clean of all superfluous material to leave only the most basic elements of human nature with which to confront this huge thing. It is a journey of roller-coaster proportions. But for now we hovered at the top of the coaster, taking the last breath of humdrum life before facing the unavoidable plunge.

In the blur of the moment I recall making coffee, and the doctor and I sat talking about… things. I was being referred to a gynae oncologist, so that side of things would wait. I do remember that the sound of a car horn, followed by the urgent barking of Tess, heralded the arrival of the mobile butcher. Like Pavlov's dog, Tess only has to hear the sound of a car horn, whether on the radio or in reality, to think that her weekly bone has arrived. She races for the door, clamouring to get outside and into the butcher's van where she helps herself to a bone from the box on the floor. If the sound has come from the radio, she stands on the empty doorstep looking confused and bereft.

This time Tess was right, and we were soon standing in the butcher's van, the doctor and I, discussing the merits of 'happy bacon'. Free-range pigs are so much more tasty than those poor crate-reared porkers and they offered a wonderfully everyday subject to discuss rather than think of the turmoil my life had suddenly become. The doctor left, 'happy bacon' in hand, and I stood in the empty, quiet cottage with this new me. This me who had cancer.

It has to be everyone's nightmare – the doctor on your doorstep, the bullet of bad news, the mention of cancer. It is like being forcibly held down and branded with a death sentence. The image of the Grim Reaper, Father Time with his 'C' shaped scythe, is synonymous with the Big C of cancer. My mother died of cancer, my aunt died of cancer, not long ago the thirty-five-year-old brother of a friend died of cancer, and her mother died of cancer. I could go on. It seemed that everyone I knew who had died, had all died of cancer; and everyone I knew who had had cancer had died. Cheery statistics. I know now that many people do recover from cancer, but this doesn't help the uninitiated and newly diagnosed.

But there were two parts to this story. Cancer was only one, and when I pushed that one aside the other word surfaced; hysterectomy. The word was so alien that in the first few days I called it a vasectomy on more than one occasion, much to people's bewilderment.

I was twenty-eight years old. Four months ago I had given birth to my first child. I had just begun my childbearing days and had already promised Barnie a brood of siblings to grow up with (finding a father was only a small hitch which could be overcome, I told him). Now, now... I couldn't think about this at all as I sat in the rocking chair rocking and hugging Barnie so, so tightly. This poor unsuspecting boy was going to get every ounce of my love, every hour of the day. I rocked and held, and rocked and held, and the tears began to fall.

THE BIG 'C'

A knock on the door disturbed me. On this one occasion I wished I hadn't left the keys in the door and in burst tomorrow's bride-to-be looking as radiant and happy as is possible. We were such poles apart, me as low as lead could take me and her floating on clouds I couldn't even imagine. I muttered something about being fine, and Betsy floated back out of the door. She brought me back to reality. Any minute I was expecting two wedding guests whom I didn't know and who were going to stay with us. Somehow I had to put all this on hold.

I chose to ignore the hysterectomy side of things because the specialists would have to confirm this anyway. But the cancer side of things I carried around with me that weekend like a new and quite radical haircut. I knew it was there, and consciously felt it from time to time. At other times I passed a mirror and saw glimpses of what it was really like. I rolled the word around in my mouth like a sweet with an unusual taste which you can't quite identify; 'cancer' and again 'cancer'. I moulded it in my hands like Plasticine, feeling it, learning its shape and texture. And each time I did, the reality sank in a little bit more and a little bit more.

Rob turned up that night with some grape medicine. He was the only person locally who knew about the diagnosis, and just knowing he knew and was there kept me going through the social niceties of the wedding on Saturday. The other thing which kept me going through the wedding of one of my best mates was a strength which I dug from the depths. It was quite a conscious thing, dressing in my finery, standing in front of the mirror, and telling myself to stand tall and proud. Amazingly, it worked. I somehow made myself feel as though I was holding some rich, rosy, cherished secret, rather than the black hole of a secret it really was.

Of course, the other thing which kept me going was my four month old son. I simply had no option but to raise my stunned body out of bed when Barnaby woke in the morning, to change his nappy when it needed changing, to feed him when he was hungry, to hug him when he was sad. On Monday morning I woke with mastitis. My boob felt like clay in a furnace and was agony every time Barnie drank. I felt lousy – fluey and shivery and exhausted. How low could I go…?

What had I done to deserve this treatment? Was there someone, somewhere, prodding needles into a doll, hating and punishing? I picked up some antibiotics from the chemist and went home to sit, shivering, in front of the fire. The tears rolled from my eyes like an unstoppable torrent. I ignored the phone and concentrated simply on getting through the day. Luckily, relief came in the form of my father that afternoon. It was good to feel his big bearlike hugs and his presence.

Two days later we were in the hospital in Edinburgh. My father, Barnie and I were ushered into a room and a female South African locum oncologist joined us. She sat down opposite me and said; 'You've got cervical cancer. You'll need a hysterectomy. How do you feel?'

I stared at her through a sudden film of tears. Was I missing something? Was a hysterectomy something that people actually wanted? Was I supposed to say 'Over the moon?' She then told me that after the operation, if I needed radiotherapy, it would affect my sex life. Sex life?! I couldn't have cared less if I never had sex again; it was like asking whether I wanted blue carpets or red. The thought of sex was so mundane when all I wanted was to live and be well.

I sensed my father bristling and wouldn't have been surprised if he had hit the lady; but he held his tongue. My father and hospitals are from Mars and Venus respectively. It was odd but like so many other times in this crazy play I had entered, my mind flashed back to memories – all of them mundane. They were my yardsticks to tell me that we were still on the same planet. This time I remembered the time my mother, father and I had sat in the headmaster's office of school number three. Headmasters' offices were much like hospitals, and my father sat there chewing gum loudly and so obviously thinking about who was going to win the 3.30 at Haydock. Here in the hospital he was with us more clearly – but he still struggled.

We got through this ordeal thanks to the inevitable passing of time and I honestly felt that I was making a mountain out of a pimple. I could have done with the script. The doctors were so cold, callous. They cannot afford to be otherwise. But one small sign of humanity sticks in my mind and was the only illustration that I was dealing with people and not robots. Just as we were leaving the room, one of the other doctors who would perform the operation placed her hand on my shoulder.

'It's OK,' she said. 'You'll be OK.'

That was all it took. It's not much to ask from anyone.

The person who really made sense was the sister of the ward I was to be on. She was the first person who allowed *me to feel the fear. It is comforting to be patted on the shoulder and told 'there there'; what helps more is for someone to recognise how you feel, allow you to feel like that, and be with you at that moment. Only then can you cease fighting and relax into the role.*

The smells in the ward, the thick air, the instruments, the trolley of pills, the tubes of blood, the catheter bags – they would all be familiar to me in time. As would that lever-of-a-chair-type-thing which lowers sick bodies into the bath. I looked at it that day and thought, 'Me? Never!' Ha ha, the gods of ill health laughed, loudly. Barnie was the one least phased by this hospital day out. For all he cared or knew we could have spent the day at Alton Towers. The rides were certainly as scary.

I had three weeks to wait for the radical (or Wertheims) hysterectomy, which involves removal of the womb, the surrounding tissue and local lymph nodes. The weeks passed like an out-of-focus film. The thing which staggered me more than anything was the depth of physical feeling involved in shock. At first there were the tears – buckets of them, lakes of them. I never imagined that I could produce so many. Like Pavlov Tess with her car horn and bone, the telephone triggered my tears. 'Bring bring' was followed by 'blub blub'. I shelved my Luddite tendencies and was delighted with a new answerphone with which I could screen all calls.

Then came exhaustion. Although I slept well, it felt as though I hadn't slept forever. The tiredness from walking a marathon a day, every day for ten months (walking Britain's coast) was remembered as a positive experience. At least physical tiredness is healed by sleep and rest; tiredness from shock is bone aching, muscle numbing, as though your body has been cast in lead then glued to the ground.

When I heard Barnie cry in the morning, I hoisted my shackled body out of bed with the sole thought of going back there as soon as possible, and by the time evening came I wondered whether I could physically hold him any more. On one occasion Barnie was in the bath and I thought I had reached the end of the road. There just seemed to be not an ounce more energy left in the tank. If there had been someone else there, I would have given up. But I couldn't.

Everyone said; 'You're strong. You'll be OK.' It was only because I had no other choice. I believe it is part of a woman's psyche to be strong and she is lucky enough to be able to draw on this when most needed. Surely this stems from her childbearing ability? You can't call a 'sicky' when you are a mother and I was like a puppet on a string in the hands of Barnie. As long as he was awake and with me, I was held upright; but when he went to bed I collapsed with the disappearance of the strings.

Bed was a dark, lonely, yet comforting cave; a wayside rest from a busy road. I felt safe here, as though if I willed hard enough I would never have to move and rejoin the highway. Of course, it was also the place where the exhaustion was happy. Sleep was still some time to come. I lay in bed feeling the haircut, tasting the word. The network of feelings which the cancer had brought on were like a tangled web in my heart and in my head. One minute I felt guilt, as though I had brought this on myself. Then I felt angry, furious at the injustice. Then I felt betrayed by my body which felt so fine but which had clearly let me down. Then I cried tears of self-pity and craved the arms of someone around me.

Every night I thought of the fate. I had become pregnant because of one irresponsible night. One night. I knew I was pregnant immediately, that night, in fact. Then the father had disappeared, and despite fierce opposition I had continued with the pregnancy. I knew now that if I had taken the other road, the supposedly 'easier' road, I could never have lived with myself. I would have just given up. It was that simple.

And there were other fateful moments. Barnie's birth had been one. I had clung tightly on to the exact memory of that night, remembering every word and smile, every laugh and touch, terrified of forgetting. I never knew why I had done that; it was almost as if I knew it would be my only experience of giving birth.

Sometimes the biggest fear of all teased out the tangle and made a straight, steel rod through my heart; What happens if I die? What will happen to Barnie? This was the one thing I kept to myself. To admit this fear, I thought, was either showing weakness or being over-dramatic. So I kept it bottled up. Dealing with people was one of the hardest things. Because death is such a taboo in this country, cancer is too. The equation cancer equals death is wrong but understandable, and I have no doubt that the Reaper and his scythe came to other people's minds. The easiest, best way to deal with this is to be entirely open. Like the time of my mother's death, and the time of single pregnancy, the unsaid words sat between me and others like a heavy cask of awkwardness. It is better if the cask is replaced with difficult words, however hard.

As time went on, I veered from wishing the operation over to simply wanting to run away. It was strange to know that I had this life-threatening 'thing' inside me, growing, mutating, eating up good cells. But I felt fine. For this reason I walked the plank as an innocent victim. If I had felt ill, things might have been easier when I woke on the day we would go to hospital. My life had been taken out of my hands and I was doing what the doctors said was necessary. I felt like a compliant puppet in the hands of my captors.

I walked a last walk around Ben's field. Tess played with sticks, and Ben followed in my footsteps. At the end of the field I wanted to keep on walking, across the ploughed and muddy field, across the newly seeded fields, into the hills – and just keep walking. Instead, I turned around, went back to the cottage, gathered Barnie's and my bag, gave Tess a big cuddle, and climbed into the car with my sister. The last time I had seen her was when Barnie was born; but life pre-cancer was already a distant memory.

One Child is Enough

Saturday 14 September

The factor in whose garden we are camped has four daughters. The youngest is maybe four-ish, the oldest ten-ish. Unfortunately they have discovered my dictaphone:

> Twinkle Twinkle little star
> How I wonder what you are
> Up above the sky so blue
> Like a diamond in the sky...

They sing – no, screech – into the machine. They are whizzing around on their bikes and playing houses in our Karrimats, making something out of nothing as only children can. They are also pushing a very startled Barnie around in the pushchair like a pet rabbit dragged from its cage and played with for a short while.

The noise levels reach crescendo but somehow Barnie manages to fall asleep in the pushchair, wrapped up, waterproofed, red-wellied, red-faced, blue-handed. He is sheltered in the garage, and the Spice Girls have been replaced by peace. Wow! I am one of four daughters. Is that what we were like?! I am already learning to see the advantages of having only one child. To begin with, an adventure like this would be impossible with a travelling creche.

When caring for Barnie, I am aware that each stage of his development is a one-off experience. Each nappy is one closer to the last one ever. Very soon, I won't have to cradle any more over-tired babies to sleep. Each day Barnie gets closer to becoming a person with whom I can reason and very soon we will be able to travel far afield again. And, of course, there won't be the added cost of more children.

This is undoubtedly my coping mechanism. 'I don't want any more children anyway,' I tell myself when I see exhausted mothers in charge of a young baby and a jealous toddler. When I see mothers struggling with huge families and top-heavy supermarket trolleys, or when I hear four screeching renditions of the Spice Girls, I think gleefully 'that will never be me!' The body and mind have clever ways of coping; if only it was like that all the time.

Friends who have children Barnie's age are now having their second and I look at their babies, any baby, and all my maternal instincts leap to attention with a magnetic power, telling me that it is time to have another. Coping mechanisms are brilliant, but they can never obliterate the lies. The truth is, I'd love a brood. Yup, perhaps even four daughters on top of Barnie. I can make such a rash statement because I know it will never be fulfilled. So I relish the peace and tell myself that one child is enough.

We woke this morning to see snow on the high hills all around and congratulated ourselves that we hadn't camped up high near Loch Builg, to wake up in a canvas igloo with only the hoofprints of a disappearing horse marking virgin snow. But really it is Ben we should be thanking for making our decision to hasten off the hills. Up a glen without a horse on a beautiful morning is one thing; in the snow is another.

The wind is icy this morning and cuts through the layers with an arctic menace, winter suffocating autumn. Barnie wears four layers on top, then waterproof dungarees over his trousers. Just as I had completed this wrapping and sent him out of the tent, he did a poo. Finding his nappy is challenge enough in the smelly, damp tent. I wrapped him up for the second time, sent him on his way, and five minutes later he had done another.

How did crofting women cope with the cold, the layers and the nappies? Their bairns were undoubtedly more hardy, but even so. And what about Eskimos? Brrrrrr. I am thinking jealously of my sister with her young children in the Seychelles.

From Invercauld (Braemar) the drovers' most direct route south would have been through Glen Clunie to Glenshee, or slightly east to Glen Isla. But the hundreds of hoofprints which once marked these routes have been obliterated by the hot rubber of incessant car tyres – rubber which once flowed from Malaysian plantations and now flows along British highways. So we have branched east along the Dee (also a route of the drovers), to pick up a track south from Ballater.

Although the Dee is also overtaken by the dreaded red road, we found a track to avoid the first part. Shielded from the main road by a large forest and a sizeable hill, the track runs along a small glen where numerous ruins indicate that this was once a thriving community straddling the Feardar Burn and its offshoots. Patches of native, deciduous woodland colour the valley sides and once offered shelter to the crofters and their beasts. The glen lay quiet except for birdsong. It felt secret, enchanted; as if, by hiding behind the folded hills, holding its breath, and staying mousey quiet, it has never been found by the tentacled roads which have probed their way into neighbouring glens.

At Inver, the Feardar Burn brought us back to the Dee and we had no choice but to walk along the main road for just over two miles. The road was blatant and rude, as unforgiving as the tarmac itself, and stripped us bare of imaginations and daydreaming. It was life's equivalent of taking an overtired toddler to the supermarket in retail rush hour. We plodded in single file; me, then Ben, then Rob and Barnie, and Tess bringing up the rear. The cars whizzed past, virtually touching Ben with their wheels and clearly ignorant of the damage he could do to their cars if he chose to swerve at that moment. Luckily Ben has plodded a long way from his wild ancestors and is quite at home on the roads.

At Crathie we joined the hoards of huddled Balmoral visitors in the car park, before crossing the River Dee on to a quieter road. It was only after that I realised how easy it was crossing this large river. To the drovers, rivers were obstacles which took thought and stockmanship. In the seventeenth and eighteenth centuries, the lack of bridges over rivers was the greatest obstacle to communication in the Highlands. Wade appeared with his military roads in the eighteenth century and built some bridges, but these weren't built with drovers in mind and were usually in the most populated areas, which the drovers sought to avoid. In fact, it appears that the drovers tried to avoid most bridges. Bridge tolls were one thing; more importantly, the cattle they drove were wild beasts used to the open hills, and the bridges in existence were narrow, wooden structures. The experience of crossing a bridge, and the sound of their hooves on the timber, would frequently make them panic, possibly causing injury to man and beast. I remember Ben's wariness at crossing the wooden bridges of the Speyside Way.

So it was that the drovers preferred to ford or swim the beasts across rivers. Cattle are strong swimmers, and, except in times of flood, the large rivers would have presented little problem. Yet it still would have taken significant stockmanship to drove several hundred cattle across a fast flowing river. Once the beasts entered the water, the drovers kept them going forwards with plenty of noise – if the leaders turned back, the rest would do the same and be in danger of being swept away.

Outside the gates of Balmoral, a small and rather forlorn open fronted shop stands alone. It is manned by two very cold ladies with dripping noses and is shaded permanently by trees which drip Scottish rain. It also houses the world's worst collection of postcards. One of the Queen and Prince Philip stands out. I wonder, have they ever walked to the end of their drive and seen this grey portrait?

For us the shop means one thing – buy! When Tess and I walked the coast, shops offered the diversion of wayside grazing in the same way Ben veers towards lush verges.

A roadside shop is a novelty which should not be missed. Chocolate beckons. This time, it is exclusive chocolate in view of the royal doorstep it comes from. No Fruit and Nut here. Barnie is still on Rob's back and munches happily, smearing chocolate art on Rob's shoulders. Tess' chocolate disappears in one go, as does Ben's. Both look to mine; 'Tough!' I tell them.

Having badgered another under-dressed, shivering American to take our photo, we set off again. So along the south side of the Dee to Cow Pat Field. The tent is erected in a small enclosure where the cattle are fed in the winter. If it rains tonight, we will wake to find we are sinking in a pool of slurry. Altogether this afternoon will not be one we remember with joy.

First it got late and we couldn't find the required, recommended farmer. Secondly there was no open land on which to camp and tether Ben, and the thought of traipsing to another farm and another would have been bad enough without a really miserable Barnie. It was only when we stopped that I realised a) he had done an inconspicuous poo which had made his bum red raw; b) he was cold; c) he was exhausted. He was simply inconsolable. Neither tent pegs nor his next favourite toy, the hammer, could cheer him up.

I changed his nappy in the biting wind while Rob put up the tent. We realised that the only thing Barnie required then was warmth and sleep. I wrapped him in his Chuckroast and held him tightly. Slowly the warmth spread through his little body from within. His face grew flushed, his hands thawed, and his breathing became regular and calm again; his innocent breath reached me.

'My little boy. I'm sorry to drag you out here on a horse in such weather.'

Then I watched and felt him sleep in my arms, peaceful at last. I felt quite depressed by this ordeal, but Rob cheered me up with a large plate of pasta, onions, herb and asparagus soup mix, and red kidney beans. We huddled in the opening of the tent.

I am now walking down the lonely road to the red phone box. It looks like the road to nowhere. These phone boxes are situated in the most remarkable places. It would be interesting to know who else stumbles across them precisely at the time when they need a phone; visitor's books, that's what they need.

Soul Searching

Sunday 15 September

Camping lost its charm this morning when the lighter fell in the meths and we had no matches. Instead of coffee and porridge we had a cold wind and smelly slurry. Barnie, ever the optimist, woke with his usual grin. He slurped several beakers of iodine purified water mixed with powdered milk and vitamin drops (a revolting concoction which Barnie drinks as thought it is the finest vintage), picked the raisins out of a bowl of muesli, and was set for another day of 'Wherever You Take Me, Mum.' Ben, meanwhile, hung his head over the fence and had 'ho hum for the life of a horse...' written across his kind face.

It took five miles of road to reach Ballater. The quiet road is lined with forestry plantations, so any views of the Dee are hidden. But the weather excluded views anyway. Somewhere up to our right, snowy Lochnagar hid under a heavy, grey quilt. The sky stayed hidden. Tunnelled in our tree-lined world, Ben was so settled that the increasingly horsey Rob led him. It was strange to fall behind and watch as an onlooker for the first time – Ben's friendly brown bottom beneath his wide load, topped with Barnie's red and blue head swaying with every stride. What freedom Ben has given us.

Nevertheless, I know everyone was pleased to reach Ballater at lunch time today, and the sense of achievement as we clopped over the beautiful old bridge into town held us bonded together with that irrepressible, contagious feel-good factor. Rob and I passed through here on several recce trips to the area, and in my heart of hearts I had doubts whether we would make it this far.

The landlady of our B&B looked askance and declared that she didn't have stables. Ben ignored her and placed his two front feet on the doorstep, much to the amusement of the accumulated party of interested people. I assured her that the local farm manager had fixed Ben up with a field, and she relaxed. She wasn't at all unnerved by the amount of saddlery and equipment which comes off Ben, and which we lugged upstairs through her spotless house. The smell of pot pourri and clean sheets was soon replaced by the smell of leather and dirty socks. Dirty wasn't the word. Rob ordered me to wash my week old socks as soon as we arrived. I then hung them out of the window and we found them later, fallen on to the cashpoint machine below. It is a well travelled sock that; a 4,500-mile-round-Britain-coastal-walk-unwearoutable sock, which I fear may have ended its days in Royal Ballater.

The B&B is pink and sumptuous. Averill was a sixty-a-day smoker and when she gave up, she took up tapestry. The walls of the house are lined with tapestries of every sort – what enormous energy has filled the void that smoking left. Of course, the very anti Rob said he would purchase some tapestries to help me give up smoking. It's not such a mad droving idea. The drovers themselves often boosted their meagre incomes by carrying home-made goods for sale in the Lowlands. This was especially true of the drovers from this part, because the knitted goods and coarse tweeds of Aberdeenshire and Morayshire were easily disposed of in the south. Haldane recounts how, at the end of the last century, drovers were seen knitting socks as they followed their beasts!

With everything dumped, we hit the pub – thirsty, hungry and celebrating. Barnie was soon playing a mean game of pool with a cue and a salt shaker, and the first pint disappeared as though the plug had been pulled. The colour rose in our cheeks. It was a matter of minutes before the ups and downs of the last few days had been pushed to the cellars of consciousness, to be replaced by only the good memories. Too cold? Nah. Ben misbehaving? Nah. Too remote? Nah. Anything suddenly seemed possible. We could carry on from here to Glen Esk, then Edzell, then Bridge of Cally, then Crieff. In fact, I think we could walk all the way back to the Borders.

We had lunch, then went to bed. All of us wearing no boots, no socks, no T-shirts or fleeces and no knickers. Clean, in a vast, clean, pink bed. The wind got up outside and blew the curtains into the room, but it didn't touch us in our bed with its starched pillows and sheets, and heavy quilt. The outside world was another world. A world we loved, but which always reaffirms the other good things in life – shelter, warmth, naked clean bodies.

Afternoon naps take me back to my childhood, with daylight shining through closed curtains and the humdrum song of daytime birds which is so different from the urgency of the dawn chorus. How strange it is that so many things we once hated are now such treats.

When I had a bath today, I saw my scar for the first time in a week. It stared up at me like the broad smile across my abdomen that it is. Like the scars in my mind which I have to learn to live with, I am learning to live with this one. In fact, I saw it in a different light today. I actually looked at it and thought; 'As scars go, it's pretty good really – pencil thin and white and fading. I must tell the consultant.' A milestone thought.

One of the things I found hardest about the hysterectomy was the severance it caused from the natural world. Females are designed for childbirth. In our wild state, all paths led to finding a mate and reproducing to ensure the continuance of our existence. The seasonal cycles reflect the cycles of the female rhythm; but now my ovaries feel dulled by their experience and, with my womb gone, removed by a knife so alien to our ancestors, I wondered whether I would ever, could ever, feel included in nature's laws.

Cancer kills in the wild. Survival of the fittest is a distant concept these days, yet this thought kept resurfacing. It felt hypocritical to talk about the bond with nature but then to run to our civilised technological advancements and the surgeon with his knife when my life was threatened. In the beginning, I was so shocked and pliable in the hands of the doctors that I thought little of any other road I could have taken. But after the operation, in the bleak moments of pain, discomfort and coming to terms with the new me, I thought often of this. Had I done the right thing? And yet, of course, I could never have refused the life-saving operation. Apart from anything, I had Barnie to live for. Sacrificing a few values is a small price to pay for my beautiful only son.

When I walked Britain's coast I felt so accepted by the land and its personalities. Silly, perhaps, but I wondered if I would ever be included again. Would I be rejected like the runt of the pack, the unfittest? This trip is doing wonders. I love to feel the elements for what they are, not seen through a window or relayed through a man with a map and remote control raindrops in a BBC studio; and to know that we have walked the country with these elements. Things haven't come full circle, because there is no going back to the person I was, but I am finding that there is still a peace in the mayhem. I may not have a womb any more, but I have a soul. And it is the soul which is me.

By Royal Appointment

Monday 16 September

Ben is Ballater's greatest football supporter at the moment. His field adjoins the playing field and so a team of sporty guardians are dedicated to feeding this poor wretch of a horse. Apparently, last night he had thirty children in his field feeding him crisps, chocolate and apples. Averill said she took her granddaughter out there this morning. 'I didn't know what horses ate,' she told us. 'So we took him a loaf of bread.'

We had a huge breakfast of bacon and eggs, which were soon liberally spread over the plush carpet by Barnie. In so many ways life on the road is hard; in others it is easy. Much of our twentieth century days are spent tidying up the mess we create in the environment we have created – both individually and globally. In the wilds, there is no hoovering or cleaning. We remove our litter, but the crumbs are left for lucky birds and beasts who are experiencing their first tastes of aduki beans and Primula.

With breakfast over, we visited Ben then set off on a lazy walk through Ballater. My socks had disappeared again from the window ledge but this time they weren't found on the cashpoint machine; taken instead on the wind to a sock graveyard. So new socks are in order, as is a fork for Barnie who is always trying to spear food with a spoon.

We purchase socks from the fishing and country shop 'By Royal Appointment to HM The Prince of Wales and HM Queen Elizabeth'. They should be blessed with blue wool at that price. I can't help wondering whether HM The Queen wears the same type of socks beneath those green wellies.

The 'By Royal Appointment to...' signs and coats of arms brand most shops in Ballater. They are worn with pride above shops like war medals on lapels. Even the chemist has one; is this where HM The Queen nips down for Colgate when Philip finishes the tube?

I like Ballater. It is a small unassuming village really, considering its royal patronage. It lies within a large meander of the Dee created by the rocky outcrop of Craigendarroch, and has spectacular surrounds – albeit largely enclosed by precisely planted platoons of pine forests. Queen Victoria certainly picked a grand spot for a bolt hole.

It has been a great relaxing day off – eating, sleeping and wandering. Rob's parents are here, in the Highlands on holiday, and they are treating us to dinner in the Craigendarroch Hotel this evening. At least I have new socks for the occasion.

Pessimism in Ballater

Tuesday 17 September

Ostracised by my smoking habit, and secretly enjoying a moment of peace, I sat on the veranda of the Craigendarroch Hotel last night, smoking a rollie and looking out to the black wet hills towards Lochnagar – and was mesmerised by their hostility as seen from the security of the hotel. Was it really possible that we had been camping out in those inky hills, alone? One little tent dwarfed by the tremendous rise and fall of the mountain waves?

Often, when you look back on something you have done, or forward to something you never know you'll do, it can seem inconceivable that you can do or did that thing. I have jumped fences on horses that would give me heart attacks now; I walked Britain's coast, but now I think 'How?'; I looked out to the wet, hostile hills and thought 'Brrr. Camping's for hardy folk.'

As I sat watching the hills it felt that something was wrong. Tess, Ben and Barnie were scattered around Ballater and I felt the distance between us all, like a mother hen who takes her brood on a walk, but turns around to find they have all wandered off; her 'home' is gone. I had a collie-strong desire to herd them all back together again! Nevertheless, I turned my back on the hills and went into Rob's parents suite in the hotel. It is the hotel where they spent their honeymoon, and Rob had given them the night as a wedding anniversary present. It is a superbly sumptuous hotel with excellent spa baths and steaks. A spoiling respite.

It is chucking it down today. A grey, miserable hill-less scene greeted us, so we have postponed departure. The route we want to take from here is as an unnamed track to Glen Tanar then the Mounth Road to Glen Esk. The Mounth Road is the highest pass in the Grampians. I have walked some of it before and know that we need ideal conditions for the exposed pass.

We were both disappointed not to get going, and a despondency set in which was aggravated by the barrier of estate factors we have come up against this morning. First I called the factor of Glen Tanar estate. We wanted to camp at the top of Glen Tanar to break up the distance between here and Glen Esk (Invermark). As the crow flies it is only thirteen miles, but involves two ascents. It would be a hefty day in one go.

Glen Tanar man did not want to know; 'I don't encourage sponsored walks,' he said. 'And if you camp there, you'll be an environmental health hazard and everyone else will want to camp there too. Besides, I'm not taking responsibility for your sixteen month old child. I would say it's not wise to bring a child of such an age into the Highlands at this time of year.'

'But,' he continued. 'I can't stop you because it's a right of way.'

'So we can pass through but not camp?' I said.

'I don't want you to, but I can't stop you,' was all he would say.

I put the phone down with mixed emotions. My initial reaction was; 'I don't want to use your glen anyway mister.' Then, like the raw nerve that it is, the other question surfaced; 'Am I unwise to have Barnie up here at this time of year?' This thought bubbles beneath the surface and emerges at the slightest criticism. Although this is only the second person to question my wisdom on this front, they have both made me think: Am I unwise?

But then you have only to look at Barnie to see how happy he is. He sits on Ben without a care in the world, unaware that these hills are potentially dangerous or that we are taking every precaution. We keep him warm and fed and safe, and we are never going to cover the remote sections of the route unless the weather is fine and settled. Surely Barnie faces more dangers at home with its plugs and flexes, cookers and fires; or accompanying me in the car on the busy roads; or in towns and cities with their people and fumes? Yet I am sensitive to such criticism. And when I think that he is my only child, the questioning seems more poignant. The thought of anything happening to Barnie is a black hole which swallows up all rationality.

When I discovered that I could never have any more children, I found myself thinking; 'If I had known that when I was pregnant I probably wouldn't have taken the bump tobogganing, or gone to Laos against the doctor's orders.'

Now I am still exposing Barnie to perils. Perhaps it is just my nature. Rob reassures me that my mad streak doesn't overflow into folly, and I trust his judgement.

So where did all this leave us? We are clearly not wanted in Glen Tanar, but there is no other way around. Neither of us want to go where we aren't wanted. So we followed a piece of advice the Glen Tanar man also gave us; 'Go to the Countryside Ranger.'

The Countryside Ranger is based opposite the B&B in part of the old station building. Here, snowed under a gastronomic spread of maps, a feast for any outdoor enthusiast, and accompanied by a large, shaggy deerhound, we found an ally. She could not have been more helpful, which, should the factor know, would probably cause him much chagrin.

We have discovered that the track we want to follow into Glen Tanar is a right of way specifically designated for horses – one of the few with such special stipulations. Why so? This first section was clearly not a drovers' route because the drovers who passed through Ballater went on down Glen Muick and then over the Capel Mounth to Glen Clova. (Much of this is no longer a proper track and parts of it are very steep, which is why we decided not to go that way.) Those drovers who came from further east followed the direct route up Glen Tanar to the point where we hope to join the glen, then over the Mounth Road. So who travelled this path with their horses, thereby handing down a horse right of way, a twentieth-century bridleway? The whisky smugglers; the ponies with their balanced barrels of whisky en route for Glen Esk.

So we know now that we can use this path, but not camp in Glen Tanar. I then rang a lady who has a horse trekking centre in Glen Tanar to find out what condition the track is in; 'Oh, it's terrible,' she said. 'There are huge drainage ditches and bogs – not at all suitable for a heavy horse and child.'

Did I detect a hint of 'keep off my territory?' The guy in the next-door outdoor shop told us it was a good path. Who are we to believe?

We have dispatched Rob into the retreating rain this afternoon on a hired mountain bike to suss out the track. At the moment it seems that everything is against us. It is the first time I have heard Rob speak with pessimism; but, as is the case with relationships, his pessimism has fuelled my optimism. We will make it to Edzell – somehow, sometime.

The land access laws in Scotland are as murky as its notorious weather. I walked Scotland's coast without really knowing what they were, always expecting someone to order me off their land and always amazed when I received a cheery greeting instead. Some people said there were no trespass laws, while others said there was simply a gentleman's agreement based on trust between land owner and visitor. In reality, the main difference between English and Scottish trespass laws is that Scottish common law has no penalty for the simple act of trespassing (unlike England), but damage or nuisance must first be proved. This is the law.

But out here, in the wide open spaces which are the Scottish Highlands, a day to day state of mutual understanding and tolerance has arisen between landowners and the public.

Rights of way are what they are – rights – and have their roots in history. Thus the whisky road. But otherwise access is on an informal basis. Footpaths and hill tracks are free for the public to use as long as they seek permission where possible, and conform to basic, courteous behaviour.*

The Countryside Ranger gave us a copy of the Concordat on Access for Scotland's hills. This sets out points of access agreed by the ten parties with interests in the Highlands, such as The Association of Deer Management Groups, National Farmer's Union of Scotland, Rambler's Association, The Mountaineering Council of Scotland and Scottish Landowners Federation. The basic agreement is that owners offer access where it doesn't impinge on management and conservation purposes, and visitors respect the needs of land management – and the livelihood, culture and communities who rely on this landscape.

The Concordat is a good agreement. In these days of step-on-my-toe-and-I'll-sue-you, it is good to see a working agreement based on trust. I wonder how long it will last?

Rob has been on his recce trip and thinks the path will be difficult for Ben. There are numerous drainage ditches, though they are only a couple of feet wide, and there are a couple of tricky burn crossings. Rob has given me exact dimensions and angles, and I've decided that Ben will make it. He will have to, because we aren't allowed to camp in Glen Tanar and the route avoiding this path would be too

---

*The route must run from one public place to another and have been used, without interruption, for a period of twenty years or more.

long for one day. Either the walk stops here or we put Ben to the test.

This afternoon I called the factor of the other estate we will be on – Glen Muick. He could not have been more accommodating. He said they were stalking, but that they wouldn't be near the track in the morning. We were welcome to use it.

So we are off tomorrow – what a big day it will be... if we make it over the ditches, burns and bogs of the whisky road to Glen Tanar.

It has been a day of highs and lows and phone calls. We are now glued to the remote control raindrops and clouds in our room. The delicious smell of leather is still with us, now joined by Ballater's best fish and chips and a bottle of bubbly to belatedly celebrate our arrival in Ballater. Perhaps romance is in the air...

Barnie and Ben, the Munro-baggers

Wednesday 18 September

A last massive breakfast, a last shower, a last clean boy. The sun sought us out through every window and the wind had run out of breath. Yesterday changed its mind to become today, the exact opposite. We were off. The distance between Ballater and Invermark may only be thirteen miles, but the same journey by road would mean a distance of perhaps sixty miles, possibly more. There is more to horse transport than the romantic image!

Ben was lying down in his field this morning and is so much more settled after two days of resting, eating and cheering on Ballater's footy youngsters. He too is re-learning the essentials in life. Either that, or the chocolate and Monster Munches have had an affect. He has been a star.

We tied Ben up to a drainpipe outside the B&B, and a crowd of people had soon gathered on the pavement. Tess, meanwhile, was loitering in the background with her 'I'm not being left behind' look on her face. Eileen was deeply concerned by Tess; 'Ohh, Tess, come here now,' she wailed every time a car came within fifty yards of her. Eileen had abandoned her cleaning duties and appeared with Averill and Margaret from the B&B, as had Teddy the fluffy white dog with an appropriate name. He loitered in the doorway, unsure about the departing guest with the extra long nose and tendency to grab anything in reach. Averill's coat got munched by Ben, as did Rob's hat – again.

'Ohh, Tess. Come off the road now,' Eileen chanted while Ben grabbed, Barnie looked at the saddle in anticipation, and we struggled with the saddling-up while being asked a stream of questions. An array of cameras stood ready.

Then Averill, who had left the remaining B&B guests to a DIY breakfast, produced Polos for Ben – ten packets. I had just bought five packets because I happened to have a pound in my pocket. Sweety snacks for horse and dog.

Finally we were packed and off, photos taken, farewells made. Ballater will never be the same again; it will always be a drove stop. We clopped back down the High Street, past flags lying limp in the still air, over the stone bridge and back to Bridge of Muick, from where we began the uphill slog into Glen Muick estate.

Ben was already dark with sweat as we started the climb. Poor lad. He had no idea of what was to come. This was just an appetiser. But he was brilliant and walked with uncharacteristically light hooves as we climbed higher and higher and the views became more and more superb – away across to Lochnagar, and down to Glen Muick, where patches of native woodland gave an indication of what much of Scotland was like before its desertification and subsequent geometric afforestation. I wondered what it was like when the whisky barrels rolled through here, before such luxuries as conservation issues were possible, when existence was everything?

We scaled the first hill easily. Ben drank thirstily from small burns, and Barnie had his in-flight drinks on board. We reached an open basin where the track became a vague path and the drainage ditches started, so we hoisted Barnie on to Rob's back and began to wend our way through the boggy basin. They say that ponies which herald from hills and moorland can sense dangerous bogs; a Highland pony would have been more suited to this terrain than a mini Clydesdale.* I could see that Ben took little notice of where he was walking, and his feet landed where they happened to land. It seemed again that I was guiding his every step. The thought of him getting stuck in a bog was always in my mind, and I stopped at every little ditch, showed him the obstacle, then pulled. Several times he lost a foot and got a rude surprise when it sank deeper than he anticipated.

*The Clydesdale Horse (described as 'the pride of Scotland') was founded in Lanarkshire (Clydesdale being the old name for the district). The breed dates back to the middle of the eighteenth century when Lanarkshire's native horses were upgraded in weight and substance by the use of Flemish stallions. Their heyday on farms was around 1911, when Scotland had around 140,000 farm horses, plus an unknown number in cities, most of which were Clydesdales in whole or part. Three years later they were serving King and Country, pulling supplies and guns in the Great War. Then came the tractor, and the Clydesdale horse was evicted from farms in the name of efficiency. In 1975 the Clydesdale was categorised as 'vulnerable' by the Rare Breeds Survival Trust. Since then, breed numbers have risen slightly and it is categorised as 'at risk.' Although Ben is only half Clydesdale, he has all their traits in miniature. They are truly gentle giants, a combination of grace and vigour, power and personality.

Yet he seemed to learn little from this lesson. I don't think the Clyde Valley taught Clydesdales much besides plodding.

Rob led us on through the boggy basin. He had had an interesting time going through this part on his bike, but had seriously underestimated Ben. Although it was hard going, it was easily possible and horses certainly went up in his estimation today. We have often talked about a two-wheel versus four-hooves challenge across country – although I have made a stipulation that the horse will be a more speedy variety than Ben.

The track swung right-handed and we dropped down into Glen Tanar. Like so many other glens, Glen Tanar was once home to a sizeable community. The ruin of Coirebhruaich was once a pub, no doubt served by the whisky barrels whose route we had just followed. Such communities would have welcomed the arrival of the drovers, who brought not just whisky and manure but also gossip and letters from neighbouring glens. We de-camped on a perfect grassy spot and I washed the sweaty Ben down in the Water of Tanar. Glen Tanar was just the most heavenly lunch spot. The damp, drizzle and cold pre- Ballater seemed impossible as I changed Barnie's nappy in glorious sunshine and he set off, hammer in hand, to rearrange a few stones and experiment with sheep shit. I actually caught him eating it the other day (rabbit droppings seem to be another favourite. He confuses them with raisins, I think).

Beyond our lunch spot, Mount Keen rose like the perfect mountain that it is – the sort of conical hill that a child might draw. Near its base, not far from where we sat, a yellow digger was working in the sunny, heathery glen.

We passed it as we began the afternoon's climb. The driver stopped to let us pass and grinned at the set up as so many other people do. 'I've seen it all now,' he declared.

I thought then about something Ffyona Campbell once said to me. I had always felt very honoured to have been helped and welcomed by so many people when we walked Britain's coast; I never knew how to thank them all. But Ffyona pointed out that perhaps, just perhaps, some of the people I had met gained something from us too – inspiration, strength, courage, humour. Perhaps, as a result of meeting Tess and I on the road, and helping us, they had set their own coastline to walk, their own journey to make. Numerous people got a good few laughs at our folly.

Recent decades have preached independence, but we can never truly be independent. We rely on each other – and by making a journey such as this you encounter and therefore rely on more people. A trust is formed. It is sad that people are now afraid of journeys because they are afraid of the very people they should be trusting. The same applies to emotional journeys, which are inextricably woven into other people's lives; every day we place or receive trust, every day we confide, we chat and we gossip. Often, one meeting leads to another and another. From time to time we meet a kindred spirit, or a friend of a friend, and claim such meetings as coincidence. We declare the world to be suddenly 'small'. Yet is it small? Do coincidences exist? Or is that just the way the world works?

I suppose that since Barnie's conception, moving to the Borders, having cancer, and then meeting Rob, I reckon that few meetings happen because the world is 'small';

few meetings happen by chance. Each step in my crazy emotional journey has been reached by the previous one. Meeting Rob was just the icing on fate's cake when I learnt, post-operatively and not long after we had got together, that he is probably unable to have children either. At first I was spooked by this knowledge. I woke up for several mornings almost afraid of what fate would offer next, into whose path would it steer me, into what pit would it throw me? I was caught on a wheel which steered one course only. How different would things be otherwise? I don't know. I can only guess at the burden I am saved; we are both saved. It is a relationship free of guilt, blame and 'if only's'. Barnie was a gift indeed.

This is just one of the reasons for enjoying the slow pace enforced by life on the road. It is easier to see through life's haze at this more gentle pace, without neon lights smeared across the speedy horizon and the forward thrust of fate's accelerator leaving me lagging behind my own life. I haven't been waking up in the mornings thinking 'what's going to happen next?', because what's going to happen next is another day on the road. The road will still be diverse with plentiful surprises, but I have been granted a little reprieve and a little perspective, an ability to stand back and see things for what they really are. Everything Rob, Barnie, Tess and I need has been carried by Ben or provided by them all: food, shelter, companionship, humour and love. The rest are trappings.

'The best things in life aren't things.' Anon.

There was absolutely nothing speedy or neon about our ascent of Mount Keen. I winched Ben up the rough, ragged path one rope's length at a time, as he stumbled and tripped, weaving this way and that from heather to boulder. We fed Ben water from the bottle and our stops became more and more frequent. Admittedly many of them were what we call Ben's 'tactical poo stops' (when he stops to release the most pathetic of droppings in the knowledge that it gives him a breather, and there is always the chance we might not notice him grabbing a quick nibble while he's there), but most stops were genuine. To Rob's amazement the sweat ran like a tap from beneath Ben's packs as we encouraged him on, as I once encouraged people who joined us for a day on the coast; 'Nearly there. Just a little bit further.' Hills are like life really. Just when you think you're getting there you realise it is only a false summit you can see, and there is still further to go.

We are here now, at our 2,500-foot summit which is the shoulder of Mount Keen, and the highest point of the journey in every sense so far. Rob has taken Barnie on to climb his first Munro, this small speck scrambling up the rocky path, and Tess, Ben and I are taking time out on the low road. I cannot even feel Ben at the end of the lead rope behind me. After the struggle to get up here we have winged feet and hooves.

The views under this watercolour sky are fantastic. The few vacant clouds are throwing their shadows over the russet hills and these, combined with the patterned effect of burnt patches of heather, give the hills texture. There are no trees to give texture. There are few burns or bogs or rocky outcrops – and the absence of all these gives this feeling of space. I could take two steps and glide, so great is the feeling of air and lightness. It is as though we are drifting on this silent air, suspended in space and time. My legs feel light and my footsteps rhythmic.

Every now and then we stop for Ben to drink from a puddle. Sometimes Tess follows his example and they drink together. Then Ben moves away to nibble at the green grass which grows around the puddles. We are in no hurry. Between them they have eaten three packets of polos since we have been up here. I feel such enormous affection for both of them and I can express this at such times of peace – a language of jobs completed, journeys taken, trials overcome. It is the language through bonding which, even in the human world, needs no vocal expression. I know that Rob and I feel closer than ever because of this silent companionship, silent language. This gem is a reward of the road and the hardships it hides.

Like the emotional effect of cancer which strips you of all superfluous material, like the clean, clear air around me now, a journey like this rids you of day to day trappings as the highs and lows teach you what it really takes to live. It is similar to looking in a mirror and seeing only the skeleton, the part which holds you up and without which you cannot hang the rest of your life upon. Not only do you see someone else in a clearer light, but you also see yourself.

I can see Rob now, walking down the hill, making his way over the boulders, dips and gullies of the path. As he comes closer, I can see the broad smile on his face and Barnie's cheery red face peering over his shoulder.

'Brilliant! What a day!' Rob exclaims. 'Unfortunately Barnie was asleep on top of his first Munro! He dropped off just after we left you and woke up just after we left the top. All the way down he's been exclaiming at the views too. He keeps throwing his arms out and going "wowowooo... oooooo!"'

That's my boy.

The Mounth Road we followed over Mount Keen was a drovers' route. The Gaelic word 'mounth' indicates a pass in this region, but strictly speaking it originated as 'monadh' which translates as moor or heath ('bealach', or 'balloch', being a pass). However, the Gaels did not give names to the 'roads' or passes, because there were none to name! The word mounth (or monadh) was applied to the whole Grampian Range, the moor; when they talked about going over the 'Mounth', they were talking about taking whatever route over the range was feasible, accessible or easiest. I guess this is why there are so many mounths now – such as Fir Mounth and Capel Mounth. The Mounth Road, being the highest and most significant, was given the name of the range itself.

To understand Gaelic would be to discover a whole new landscape. So many of the geographical features are given meaningful names, translated from Gaelic to become stonemasons hill, hill of the black pig, gloomy hill, the complainer. I only know this because Rob is a self-confessed Munro-bagger. He has books and maps and tables of all the known Munros.

The Gaelic names of the mountains sound musical and romantic, but, when translated, not all are quite so romantic. Some are simply practical – greenish grey hill, greenish grey bare hill, etc. I could imagine this landscape being sung into existence as Australia once was by the Aborigines.

Rob is pretty good at singing the path into existence ahead of us. We rolled down from Mount Keen, Ben's packs adding momentum to his already swaying motion so that it must feel to Barnie as though he is on a ship in a storm. Unlike Barnie, who has never had a security blanket (other than Tess), Ben must have something in his mouth. He clutched at my scarf all the ay down like a child with a 'going home present'.

South-facing Glen Esk opened out before us, funnelling us down to the kind valley with its pasture and sunshine. At Glenmark there is a perfect cottage used for holiday lets, and nearby is the Queen's Well where Queen Victoria and the Prince Consort stopped to quench their thirst after having climbed Mount Keen (and slighted Tomintoul). Albert died a few weeks after drinking from the well (was the fever a result of the water?). The puddle of water, now enshrined in a stone crown-like edifice, certainly looks pretty murky, and a memorial reads; 'Rest, traveller, on this lonely green, and drink and pray for Scotland's Queen.'

The words of so many protective factors rung in our ears and we resisted the temptation to stop and camp here. Instead, we followed the Water of Mark down here to Invermark where the Mounth Road stops and the tarmac road begins, and where I already knew that we had a field for Ben and an ally with a patch of lawn to camp on. Bea welcomed us with a broad smile and a tray spread with a white napkin, a pot of tea, china cups, a jug of milk and home baked biscuits. She runs a B&B here at the House of

Mark, which was also once a pub. So we are camped in her garden while Ben grazes a riverside field. Bliss, and a huge and all consuming sense of achievement.

Dreaming of Hills

If you could physically extract elements of the human character, the entrance to hospitals throughout the world would be lined with people's Dignities, hung up on arrival to be rescued on departure. On my first day, before I had even had the operation, I was made – and I mean made – to travel by wheelchair to the x-ray department. Apparently I was now hospital property and they didn't want me tripping up on a stretcher or prosthesis, hurting myself, and suing the hospital for millions.

So I was wheeled ceremoniously along the impersonal corridors while trying to hide under a blanket and forget the fact that I had ever walked Britain's coast. It is quite amazing what you will let people do to you. This thought came to me time and again over the next week: Did I really need to wear those sexy, skin tight, knee-length white pop socks (to stop clots), or was this a hospital policy to keep the medics amused? If they had told me to wear a boob tube (good for stimulating lung capacity), I probably would have complied. What trust we place.

I had been in hospital for well over twenty-four hours before the operation came around. Supermarket Sweep was on TV. Women were answering questions, winning seconds then minutes to spend in the supermarket acquiring goods, the height of consumerism relayed to the nation. I remember it well because I had expected the world to stop just now, to stop and wait for me. Then the ward Sister, Eunice, walked in and Barnie, lying on the floor, grinned at her, and I went back to the room with Eunice and prepared to take the pre-med. But panic welled up inside me in an overwhelming desire to run out of the hospital. I couldn't do this.

'You can,' the wonderful Eunice calmed. 'I know you feel well enough, but you need this operation. We'll all be here for you.'

She hugged me tightly. Even then, even as I swallowed the sleeping pill, I thought; 'I'm going to wake and find this was all a big mistake.' You cannot switch off denial.

I lay back with Sgd Ohamn playing through earphones, and thought of my little cottage with its cheerful fire, its spirit, now gone cold because I wasn't there. I thought of the cold grey ash in the numb hearth. I looked at the window and through it to the wall outside, and could see enough to know that it was getting dark in a grey dreary way that only British winters know. The hospital was unnaturally bright and light. I could hear the continual stream of footsteps up and down the corridor outside, busy, no-nonsense, metronome footsteps. My spirit felt empty, completely void, as though I had left it behind too, back in the little cottage with the burnt out fire. The fire was my spirit. As long as it was out, my spirit was out. I thought of the moment it would be re-lit, but I felt too sleepy then. By the time I went to theatre, I didn't care about anything.

I know people have hysterectomies every day, but I am telling you all this because it was a first for me. Imagine when operations to remove the womb were first carried out. Now... pff... how easily a word such as hysterectomy is bandied about, mentioned in passing to be easily forgotten.

I woke with part of me missing and I didn't like it. Admittedly, in the beginning, most of my time and energy was spent pressing the self-regulating intravenous morphine button as a child might ceaselessly flick the TV remote control buttons, channel surfing. I didn't particularly want to feel this new body. I knew there were two jam jar drains, one each side, and a catheter bag, because every time I moved they got in the way. But I certainly couldn't get myself to feel or look at the wound. When I did finally feel it, I ran my fingers over the staples which pulled the wound together and counted them with a sudden intrigue. I had heard of keyhole surgery, and honestly imagined I would have a wound no longer than the width of my hand, not the thirty odd staples which held my abdomen together. I had never bargained on being a punk, and hoped in that moment that they wouldn't leave any behind – so that next time I went through the airport security I would go 'bleep'.

I had the operation on the Tuesday. On Wednesday I was hoisted up, gingerly placed in a wheelchair, taken to the bathroom and lowered into the bath in the chair-lever-type-thing. The next day I told myself that if I could walk Britain's coast, I could jolly well walk to the bathroom, at least one way. The walk, witnessed by a ward of middle-aged and elderly ladies recovering from pelvic floor repairs and '-ectomies' of various kinds, was the most memorable

I have taken. Nothing in my life had ever prepared me for this. A sign above the exit door said, in bold letters, Walk Tall. I could hardly walk, dammit, and when I did it was with my nose hovering inches above the shiny, stinking hospital floor.

All this was carving a deep, non-replenishable groove in my psyche. I had walked Britain's coast with such ease and ignorance, marvelling at so much yet never appreciating the central focus of the trip – walking. I vowed, during those painful trips to the bathroom, that I would never take walking for granted again. I vowed too that one day I would look back and laugh. Humour was outwardly elusive because my monkey muscles, the ones which ache wonderfully when you really laugh, had been cut in half. I had no choice but to be outwardly serious, but humour was there in my imagination and I saw myself shuffling down to the shops with my plastic handbag of pee swinging from one hand and my lower legs enclosed in their tight white pop socks, the height of hospital fashion.

Wind was the other thing which threatened my serious countenance, and when a friend witnessed my genuine excitement at my first post-operative fart I had to order him not to laugh. Wind was a deadly serious matter. I had been pumped up with air during the operation but then denied the ability to release it. Being unable to fart is as painful as being unable to laugh – more so. Each tiny poop was a relief and achievement.

Barnie had been staying with Charles and some friends in Edinburgh, and rejoined me in hospital on Thursday. I was determined to continue breastfeeding him throughout this ordeal. Luckily, everyone involved complied with my wishes because I wasn't strong enough to face things without him or strong enough to fight for this privilege.

A lady from Simpsons Maternity hospital had been helping me through the period of not feeding Barnie. Leslie had the title of 'Breast Feeding Specialist' but was more of a milk maid to me; for two days she appeared morning and evening, pump in hand, and through this and sheer determination my milk still flowed, albeit weakly. I lay on my side, put a pillow over my wound, and fed Barnie. Then, that side done, someone took him and I rolled over to feed the other side. It took time, but it was something I could do when I couldn't even cuddle my first and only son.

As the days went on I would try to get Barnie up and dressed before my next sister, PC, arrived to take him out for the day. Every day was the same. The battle to complete this small task left me exhausted and utterly despondent. I shed tears every day, but never learnt. I'd try again the next day and the same thing happened.

Being unable to care for your own child is like trying to tell yourself you don't need sleep. Barnie was only four months old and my hormones ordered me into action; when I saw the nurses and my sisters holding him and making him laugh, my heart cried and I felt as useless as an empty hospital bed. I held tightly on to the sometimes invisible thread which linked me with the future, and the minutes, then hours, then days passed thanks to the relentless clock hands, and all the time I kept my eyes and hands on my 'Little Bag of Outside', which a friend had given me. It sits by me now, the green paper bag holding acorns, fir cones, *some feely pebbles, beech nuts and conkers. I looked at photos of the hills and reassured myself constantly that the hills, like the future, were waiting for me.*

I say that animals remind me to enjoy the here and now, not to be so wrapped up in the future or the past, but now I needed the future. So how do sick animals cope? They don't tell themselves there will be infinite bunnies to chase in the future or shady fields with lush pastures to graze. Instead, their stoicism comes from the knowledge that if they display weakness through illness they will probably get eaten. Some farmers say that a 'sick sheep is a dead sheep' because by the time they display sickness they are past curing. Some people are the same, and we all have an inherent survival instinct; but on the whole we have lost that necessity for stoicism in the absence of predators, and gain our endurance through holding on to the future and all that it has in store.

The results from the operation came through after a week. They had found part of one lymph node to be cancerous and told me I would probably need radiotherapy. But I couldn't have cared less what they were telling me. Once again, my body took control and told me how to handle this situation. It said, 'Put off everything till tomorrow.' I knew that I needed to get perspective back into my life before thinking about anything else. My body said 'One day at a time. Wait until you feel strong enough physically before coping with this next blow.' In one large way I had been severed from the animal world. Survival of the fittest means that I wouldn't have survived in the wild; yet in other ways I was discovering so many hidden depths to this body and mind I had taken for granted for so many years. Now, my body said one thing was of paramount importance – 'Get Home'.

Our hospital room was full of flowers, mostly lilies. For a week their pure white forms and strong smell had sat on the murk of disinfectant, sick bodies and hospital food like brilliant water lilies on a revolting, oily pond. They were great at the time, adding beauty to the room, but when PC loaded them into the pram to take to the car I knew that I didn't want them anywhere near me. The smell and sight of them represented the womb I had lost.

I hung some clothes on my bony frame, picked up my tatty Dignity by the door, and was soon being driven out through the snowy streets of Edinburgh. People scurried here and there, trying to dodge the flakes, and the hundreds of thousands of megawatts of electricity which keep Edinburgh alive burnt bright through the greyness. I sat very still in Rob's car, with Tess' warm snout resting on my shoulder, watching all this and listening to music and wondering again how it was that everyone was so busy getting on with their lives.

Hospital life freezes you to a senseless being. I had to revert back from a horizontal body on a bed to a person who feels and sees and wonders. It wasn't till I got home, back to the cheerful little sparky spirit of the cottage, that I felt a little more whole. The Macmillan Nurses funded someone to come and care for Barnie (and me) for the next four weeks. Susan was a local girl who had travelled extensively and had developed six arms and 360 degree vision because she normally had umpteen children in her charge. One small boy, a dog, a horse and a sick mother were a pushover, but she very quickly became an important person to me in more ways than caring. Nothing was too much. In fact, it wasn't long before I had to wait for her to be out of the house before I could sneak outside and stagger round the corner to feed Ben his hay and nuts. I dreaded being caught and scolded.

Over the next month, Susan kept the spirit of the cottage alive – both figuratively and actually. I will remember her cheery face framed by curly hair as she battled out into the cold with Barnie to gather 'sticks' – a curious Borders expression for hefty great logs; or the way she taught Barnie to 'clap' Tess (another interesting Borders' expression meaning 'stroking' the dog!).

I will also remember her support when, after three days at home, I went one hundred paces backwards and felt terrible. It became apparent that I had an infected clot. The pain came in excruciating spasms which left me hunched up in a tiny ball. I felt sick and faint every time I got up. Luckily, morphine arrived the night it got that bad and gave me the curious sensation of painless pain. The next day Rob took me back to the hospital and we were told that, because only part of one lymph node had been affected, the radiotherapy decision was borderline. Radiotherapy to the abdomen can damage the bladder and bowel. It will, as I knew, affect your sex life and zap your ovaries (which I was delighted to have hung on to). Radiotherapy would be an insurance policy, but possibly unnecessary and harmful. While some doctors would have recommended it, mine didn't. The decision was ultimately mine, and one which wasn't hard to make. We went home ecstatic.

Four weeks would bring us to Christmas. I fixed this time in my head like a goal post; when I passed through it, I thought, life would return to normal. Everyone had told me that I 'would breeze through the operation', would 'be back on my feet in no time.' So I felt I had to live up to this. But the infection pulled me down. This undoubtedly set me back and back – and ultimately infringed on the psychological heap which had been stored in cerebral cellars. When my brain said 'hey! It's time to cope with this heap,' my body was still struggling. In many ways, by the time Christmas came I had overcome the easy part.

Dreaming in Hills

Thursday 19 September. Day off.

For months Barnie has scrabbled about on his hands and knees in the dirt, but now he is upright, homo sapiens in the full. Walking is still tentative, though, and falls are common as he explores Bea's garden and searches for balance on slopes and stones. I have found, through this amateur walker, a cultural link with Asia – hunkering down.

In China, you don't stand and wait for a bus, you sit on your haunches and take the weight off your legs. Well, when you have spent all morning walking and wish to sit at lunchtime but can't because of the amateur walker, you hunker down wherever he is. You can't sit down because you will have to get up every few minutes. Hunkering is the answer. And what if it's wet and you want to sit down but have neither a seat nor waterproof trousers? Like waiting for a bus in the monsoon season, or in the middle of the night when Ben is being silly on his tether chain and you are trying to talk some sense into him? You hunker. It is actually comfortable for long periods of time now. I can't wait to try it in the post office queue or the supermarket, or in the sometimes interminable hospital waits.

Rob is sleeping in the sun. He only managed a couple of pages of his book before his sleep switch flicked – in true Rob fashion. Doctor's fashion probably. No nestling down, letting the events of the day wash over him, worrying about something. One minute awake, the next asleep. I am jealous and tired, and will probably be exhausted by the end of this trip. This is a good tiredness. It is a tiredness cured by sleep and not the paralysing tiredness of shock or deep despondency or working night and day to fight off demons.

When Ffyona Campbell finished her epic walk and said to the cameras, 'Don't let the bastards grind you down,' I imagined she was referring to the press who had plagued her throughout. But now I know it was the demons. During an endurance walk, as in life, you are plagued by demons of Worry, Doubt and Fear. I thought of this in my lowest low, after Christmas, when my body still struggled and my mind grappled with this person post-cancer who was trying to rediscover an elusive life. It was a time when I sat back and thought, 'Walking Britain's coast was a trip of a lifetime, yet every single day people undertake journeys of far greater more significant proportions, silently, patiently, possibly painfully.'

So much of the time we are oblivious to each other's journeys. We ask each other 'how are you?' on the telephone and face to face, and we expect the answer 'fine' or 'great'. If you have a cold you may say 'a little under the weather,' but if you are tired of fear, depressed, frightened, lonely; if you are under the weather psychologically the veneer of stoicism so often glosses over how you feel. Yet our only predators are our full lives, precious time and TVs – all of which make it so easy to ignore the way we really think or feel.

Here I am, in among those hills I dreamt of as I clutched my Little Bag of Outside and my plastic handbag of pee and told myself that the time would come. We are having a brilliant day of dreaming and pure relaxation in our outdoor home. We entertained Bea to coffee on our Karrimats (although she provided the coffee, in china mugs, and home-made biscuits). Anyone who makes it fifteen miles up Glen Esk, to the end of the road, deserves to discover her wonderful spot and delicious biscuits.

Invermark consists of a small cluster of dwellings, a church and the basic remains of a sixteenth-century castle which was built to guard the vital pass from Glen Esk to Deeside (which we have just negotiated). The shell of the castle tower, now surrounded by scrubby trees and visited by ambling tourists, seems so peaceful and non-violent.

In the afternoon, once Barnie and I have also slept, we wander up the edge of Loch Lee into Glen Lee. The loch is brown and so still, and way above five buzzards circle on thermals, filling the glen with their plaintively eerie calls. At the end of the loch, craggy outcrops adorn the glen sides and add a West Highland feel. It is only when you look back beyond Invermark and see the distinctive geometrically-patterned bellies rising and falling so smoothly that you remember where you are. These patterned hillsides are so typically Grampian, and illustrate the extent to which grouse shooting reigns as business. The heather is burnt rotationally in these blocks because young grouse thrive on young heather shoots, while high heather is essential for its insect life and for breeding. This is extensive management.

We have been putting up grouse all along our route, sending them up with their rather staccato hysteria, and we have passed rows and rows of shooting stands (butts). The Grampians are more tamed than I imagined – if the word 'tamed' can still be applied to hills which throw down their mists and rain and snow with scant regard for predictability.

Under today's sunshine it is hard to imagine any other scenario. At the top of Glen Lee we have found the Falls of Unich and Rob is swimming – brave, mad, and cleaner than us. We have found a hidden little gem of a glen, and Rob has fulfilled a promise he regularly made to me before there was any romantic involvement between us and at a time when I was low and weak; 'The hills are there waiting for you,' he used to say. 'There's so much to explore, so much to do together. Remember that.'

Chaos at the Retreat

Friday 20 September

'Away to the west where I'm longing to be, Where the beauty of heaven sweeps down to the sea, Where the sweet scented heather blooms fragrant and free; On a hill top high above the dark island...' Rob sings us around the Hill of Rowan with its grassy track meandering through the heather... the same verse over and over, but we don't mind.

On top of the hill is a memorial monument, conical, like an upside down ice cream cone, and beside the path is an ancient stone etched with a barely discernible cross. This is Drostan's Cross and the Latin cross is apparently typical of Columbian church style, though a combination of an amateur eye and centuries of weather erosion give it the appearance of a weak cross on a fallen boulder. Local legend says that King Robert the Bruce planted his royal standard on the stone before a battle to quell the Earl of Buchan in 1306.

We emerge back on the single track Glen Esk road at the hamlet of Tarfside. Tarfside school is on lunch break and its fifteen odd pupils flock to the wall to feed Ben tufts of picked grass, chattering incessantly. We eventually have to drag Ben away from such attention and find our own lunch spot.

A mile down the road is The Retreat Museum, now thrown into disarray by an un-tethered horse and a free-range toddler, whose digestive system is coping with oat onslaught. Children and animals... exasperation and humour. We unload Ben outside the cottage-turned-museum, tether him on their rough patch of lawn, tie Tess to the bench, and go into the museum. No sooner have we entered the museum, when Barnie does a poo. I go back outside to give him his alfresco change, only to see Ben making a bid for freedom, wandering off down the road dragging his tether chain. Tucking hefty Barnie under one arm I set off in pursuit, while Tess causes uproar from her bench thinking that we were leaving without her. I retrieve Ben, tuck fifteen feet of chain under one arm, re-hoist Barnie with the other, and walk back to the museum.

Rob is still in the museum, marvelling at life before Pampers, and I am being watched through the window by various amused museum attendants. Rob has reappeared, Barnie is changed, Ben is re-tethered and we have decided to see the museum one by one. No sooner does Rob disappear for the second time than Ben again pulls his pin from the sodden ground. I leave Barnie with the laughing museum janitor, retrieve Ben again and come back to find Barnie abandoned in favour of some scarce visitors and Tess well wrapped around the bench. Giggles well up through exasperation. I have rolled myself a cigarette and decided to sit and let the events of the day wash over me.

Caring for children and animals is a little like sweeping an earth floor. Just when you think everything is fine and settled, swept and happy, it all starts again. How easy it is to while and will away your child's development. Barnie's birth was a mistake – the best one I ever made; but it wasn't a conscious decision. I never really thought what it would be like to have a child, never read any books, and certainly never appreciated just what a full-time job motherhood is.

'Let's get single mothers back to work,' the politicians say. Well, I say let them do what they are best at – look after their own children rather than pass them on to someone else, ensure that they have the best possible childhood – because surely the best mother is the mother? While I can fully understand why many mothers need to work, and others want to work (who wouldn't want to escape a toddler's tantrums from time to time?); let those who *want* to be mothers, be mothers. Single motherhood, motherhood for anyone, is hard enough without Westminster suits applying pressure, making you feel guilty for being employed in such a vitally important and anything-but-easy job.

Barnie is now making earth castles on the lawn. He is so intent on his little job and so ignorant of the broader scale of things. At the moment he is part of the free, wild ocean but it won't be long before he finds himself channelled gradually into the estuaries of experience, probably cynicism. Long may he retain aspects of that free ocean.

I love museums such as The Retreat. It is through them that the reality of crofting lifestyles, of life in the Highlands, and of the impact of the Clearances, comes alive. Squeezed into one small 'black house' was an entire crofting family and often their beasts too. They shared accommodation with bairns and whisky stills alike. In one room, the family cooked, ate, washed and slept. What a hard existence it must have been; yet this was before the days of mass communication, when hardship and problems were an accepted element of life and there were no media or advertising moguls to preach the unnatural ethos that all of life is happy – brilliant white teeth and perpetual sunshine. It was before the days of choices, when survival was everything, and, if you had cancer, you died.

The thing which amazes me about such crofting recreations is that the women wore white. Bleached, starched, white pantaloons, dresses and aprons hang from clothes hoists above unlit peat fires with their black kettles. How many hours must have been spent washing! Even in this age of Daz and Persil it is hard to keep white white. Then there are spurtles. These are wooden utensils used for stirring porridge and were therefore an important part of a crofting kitchen. A whole wall in The Retreat was filled with spurtles of every size and shape. Often, they had beautifully handcrafted wicker handles of various patterns, each one a functional work of art. Some handles were heart-shaped, and these were given as gifts to sweethearts.

The Retreat Museum is packed solid with all sorts of goodies. The first thing I saw was a Bronze Age dagger found on the Hill of Rowan. Even from the map it is evident that Glen Esk has been inhabited for years; there are barely discernible field systems, cairns and cross stones. The Glen is a museum itself for those who wish to fossick among the heather rather than within walls. It is easy to see why this glen has been so inhabited over the years. It is south facing, well sheltered, well watered, and close to the lowlands and the coast. Over the years it has been the scene of mining (copper, lead and alabaster), and the route of drovers and troops alike. So secret is the glen that a leading Jacobite, the Laird of Balnamoon, hid in a cave here for many months after Culloden and was never found. When he finally emerged he was granted a reprieve. The Retreat is well named.

When I emerged from the museum it was 4 p.m. and, although we had only walked four miles, it was time to find somewhere to camp. As usual, the excitement of uncertainty and not knowing where we would be in an hour was mixed with the maternal worries of getting Barnie fed and slept. We are in the land of large estates which are like distilleries in that they are manned by people you never see.

A friendly man appeared from the house neighbouring The Retreat. 'What a fine horse,' he said. 'But I want to ask you a question. How much does it cost to keep a horse?'

'You see,' the man went on. 'I work at the top of the glen and have often thought that it would be more sensible to ride to work, especially in the winter.'

The man listened politely while I weighed the advantages of no MOTs or breakdown recovery against the disadvantages of shoeing fees and ploughing through winter mud with bundles of hay, while his daughter, Elara (named after one of the moons of Jupiter), continued to stroke Ben's coat to a smooth sheen. It was obvious that, whether or not he wants a horse, this was an original method of introduction. No weather speculations here.

'Well, you must camp here tonight. Ben can graze the lawn,' Eric said.

I looked over to the small lawn crammed with honking geese and broody chicks and startled ducks being bossed around by both, and I knew that two circuits of it with Ben's hooves would put Eric off horses forever. So the elusive factor was contacted and Ben is grazing the neighbouring field. But Old Macdonald never mentions excrement – the garden, which looked so homely with its fowls from a distance, is quite another thing to camp on. Interesting ground sheet, interesting smells on our 'pillows'.

We were saved from having to cook among fowl shit, and Eric, Cathy and Elara welcomed us into their homely, steamy kitchen where a of pair of budgies slept silently under a coat draped over their cage and a content cat fried gently on the aga. The conversation flowed in the company of this warm couple. Cathy is opening a little linen shop next to their house, from where she will also sell her home blown, lace-covered geese eggs. They are quite unique; and certainly unique to the glen with its farming generations.

It was clear that the couple relished visitors – hence the novel introduction. They moved here from the Wirral some years ago and spoke of how hard it is to be accepted in such a glen; a community where several generations of your family need to have lived before acceptance is even contemplated. As we chatted, the temperature plummeted and I couldn't relax. Ben's field was huge and littered with trees, tree stumps, bogs, burns, rusty wire, corrugated iron, a burnt out caravan and goodness knows what else. When I left the warm kitchen and went to check on Ben after dark I found him racing around all this in search of security. He was sweating profusely and the steam rose off him into the icy night. I noticed too that he had had a tussle with some rusty wire on his back leg. It hadn't broken the skin, but there was the red stain of wire. I felt sure that if he didn't damage himself on some hazard, he would catch a chill when he eventually calmed down. From there I checked Barnie who was home alone in the tent on the fowl shit. He was well wrapped up in his Chuckroast and slept soundly, despite the fact that by 9 p.m. there was ice on the tent.

Back in the kitchen, I listened half-heartedly to the conversation and joined in intermittently, but my thoughts were really outside with Barnie in the tent and Ben in the field. Everyone expressed concern, then quickly got back to the subject in debate. Only a parent can feel such weighty responsibility, and it reminded me of so many occasions in the cancer journey; I had wonderful friends who listened sympathetically when I talked about the post-operative pain or the fear, but things invariably moved on to other topics. Like responsibility, you cannot turn off pain or fear. Whatever support and help I received from people around, only I could deal with these things. You can gain strength from others' words and actions, you can be helped by professionals, you can be helped in helping yourself – but you can't pass the problem on to anyone else.

Perhaps this is why people emerge stronger from life's trials. The more you dig, the stronger you get. I remember the words of Marion, the local minister at home; 'You get strong by knowing your own weaknesses.' And in getting stronger, you become more whole, because surely a whole person is someone who acknowledges they cannot always be strong? By walking Britain's coast I became strong in people's eyes. From then on people said to me; 'You'll cope. You're strong.' But I was as weak as anyone else. During the cancer ordeal I wanted to tell these people that they were wrong. I was terrified. I wanted to call for help, but couldn't find the right words – and life has to go on. Instead, I began to find a voice for my weaknesses. A plant which takes root on a windy island realises its danger and digs its roots deeper. The wind doesn't necessarily stop, and the plant doesn't cease struggling, but it has become a little more adept at coping with the onslaught.

Responsibility, like 'coping,' can feel overwhelming. When I became a single mother, I often looked at conventional 'mother/father' families and realised that very often the mother was single anyway; father was away at work and played a small role (if any) in actual caring. The difference is in responsibility. Regardless of how many nappies a father changes or doesn't change, he surely feels bound by conscience, love, duty – whatever: single motherhood means single responsibility more than single caring. All obligation, nurture, support and love flows from one source. Sometimes I look ahead to the many many years ahead with Barnie, helping him to set out on the river of life with its meanders and rapids, and feel daunted by the enormity of the task. Mindfulness. I remember this and, although it is not always easy, I bring myself back to the present and each day as it unfolds.

Turning the Corner

Saturday 21 September

A hefty clout from Barnie's beaker of milk this morning, and the usual friendly nip from Ben, assured me that both were fine – despite the ice inside the tent and the fact that it dropped to minus 5°C last night. We went to the tent with hot water bottles, and I slept with all my clothes on. Barnie, sleeping between us, woke at some hour of the night and I had to sit up in the cold air and cuddle him back to sleep again, jealously wishing that they made Chuckroasts for thin-blooded adult campers. Unless the weather cheers up we will not be going further than Edzell. Luckily we had the warmth of Eric and Cathy's kitchen to take refuge in this morning.

The flimsy material of the tent may offer little warmth on such a night, but it is something. The drovers slept out every night, wherever they were and whatever the weather, sheltered from the elements by nothing more than the contents of the ram's horn and their plaid, (a long, broad, tartan, woollen cloth which was originally the sole article worn, but is now draped over kilts in 'traditional' Highland dress). I read in one source that the drovers sometimes kept warm by dipping their plaid into a nearby burn and letting the sodden wool freeze around them, thereby forming a sheltered igloo.

The drovers' dress was made up almost entirely of such woolly garments. One description of late nineteenth-century drovers in Haldane reads; [the drovers were] dressed usually in homespun tweeds which smelt of heather and peat smoke and which were so thick that those who wore them looked like bears as they lounged heavily along; 'great stalwart, hirsute men' they were 'shaggy and uncultured and wild,' their clothing and physique alike suited to the hardship of their lives.

The drovers sound like terrifying men, yet Haldane and other literature agree unanimously that they were both remarkable and remarkably honest. There were two types of drover; one who brought and drove cattle for either farmers or capital rich gentry, and the other who brought cattle for themselves and speculated heavily. Either way the drovers had to be businessmen, possibly haggling over prices before setting off with their hundreds of beasts in the knowledge that even a couple of lost cattle could seriously reduce any profits. Then the drovers had to ensure that their animals reached the market by a certain date without actually hurrying them, and thereby jeopardising their well-being. The drovers therefore carried, in their beasts, the honour of those for whom they drove. Sometimes the farmers had parted with their cattle with only the written or spoken promise of future payment. The drovers who violated their word, their honour, would not find future work easily. As the droving trade flourished, reputation was everything.

The sun appeared like an understanding friend, and we packed up while Ben caused great consternation in the fowl's yard and was fed bread crusts and cauliflower leaves by Cathy and Elara. Barnie's packing hasn't improved and, unless we are quick, he unpacks as fast as we pack; the powdered milk scattered like bird food, the soup packets chewed, the oatcakes each missing one nibble, and a few undesirable extras placed in the packs to be found later.

Our packing up hasn't got any quicker either, but it is methodical. It is amazing how one seeks ritual and routine while camping as one does in a house, even more so. The tent pegs live with the cutlery, and the hoof pick lives in the outside pocket along with Polos. My backy lives with the paperwork and woe betide anyone who moves it. Everything in our transient home has its place and structure. Potential for domestic quarrels? Possibly. My orderly chaos versus Rob the Boy Scout with his umpteen plastic bags. (How many people move into a new house complete with a plastic bag collection?) But we work well together and I am very aware that Rob is leaving tomorrow and we will be joined by Sophie, a great girlfriend of mine. I know it will be difficult for both of us – for Sophie because it is hard to enter something like this halfway through and our routine will seem pernickety, and for me because I will miss Rob enormously.

Cathy and Elara waved us off and we followed the winding, wooded road through slender birch trees resembling densely packed pins in a pin cushion. Their soft purple branches hung still in the sunshine, autumn sunshine with winter promise, and cast dappled shadows on to the road and pasture below. The continuous sound of running water and darting bird song were backing to Ben's hooves on the tarmac. After two miles we found a bridge over the River North Esk and are now walking along its south bank, following the original road which is now a good path through amazingly lush fields grazed by sheep. It is surprisingly warm today after the cold of last night.

Cattle grids separate the fields which are squeezed into the bottom of the river valley, and we are channelled through the adjacent gates. But as we get further down the glen, the heather sides drift apart as if releasing us from their grip and allowing the fields more room. At a farm called Holmhead, we swing right and are facing the entrance to the glen. Suddenly there are no hills on our horizon; instead there are pylons – *muckle** great steel ones guarding the entrance to the glen.

As we pull up at an old ruin for lunch, a wood ahead conveniently hides the pylons and the sun is casting shadows which creep slowly over the receding hills, changing their colours constantly; orange bog grasses, green reeds, rubbles of grey rock, autumnal hills splashed with late heather. Now bright under sun, now dark under cloud. This is the backdrop to our last lunch together and there is a sense of clinging on to this time as though, if we do not fully appreciate the day, the winds of change will blow again and destroy this sense of oneness.

The ruin is a basic one, but after the recreations of The Retreat it is easier to imagine that the deep room was a

*Muckle – Scots word for huge. Wonderfully onomatopoeic.

cellar which possibly hid whisky or Jacobites, and that the biggest area, now filled with fallen stones and spongy grass, was the hearth of the cottage where the spinning wheel and cradle sat alongside the fire. A single ash tree stands at the corner of our grassy clearing and looks as though it hides a chest of treasure beneath its roots. Ben is dozing on his tether chain, and, while I accompany Barnie on his explorations, I can see Rob lying in the sunshine, looking up to the sky and thinking of going 'home'. It seems strange to call it home because at the moment 'home' is right here, under the ash tree beside the ruin. We have spent the same time on the road as we have in our new cottage, two weeks, but even if we had lived there longer I would feel the same. Home is the journey.

Lunch is oatcakes, cheese spread and dried apricots. It has occurred to me that Barnie's diet is similar to Dervla Murphy's when she went from Ireland to India on her bicycle – powdered, skimmed milk and dried apricots. He is following in good footsteps; though I am sure that by the time he is ten he will hate horses and the outdoors and spend his time slouched in front of the TV.

Edzell isn't quite the exotic town of travel books, where crumbling architecture is admired by weary travellers who congregate, jubilant or pensive, full of stories and thoughts, to sit in cafes soaking up the culture and meeting eccentric individuals of imaginative proportions. It is a one street agricultural town at the mouth of Glen Esk. It has a Spar shop and a newsagent and two hotels, and is exactly ninety miles from Aberlour when following drovers' routes. Edzell is a name familiarised to us through planning of this walk, like Dogger, Fisher and German Bight are to radio listeners, and who wouldn't be delighted to visit Dogger or Fisher? On arrival in Edzell, a park on the right was filled with mothers and children, picnickers and dog walkers. There were swings and slides and bins for dog excrement. Seeing all this was like moving back from imagination to reality, waking up from a dream. Tomorrow I will take Barnie to the swings and he will become a child of the era once more.

There is a wedding on in Edzell this weekend and all four B&B's and one other hotel are full. The only hotel which had rooms, in plenty, is this one, set back off the main street behind a car park of inverse proportions to guest numbers. It is as grey and dreary as the most *dreich* * of Scottish days. Inside is no better. In fact, it is hard to believe that such a hotel can still exist, except perhaps in a Bill Bryson book.

The entrance, facing a residential street where houses with names such as 'Du Poppin' indicate that life is basically quiet, pretends to be grand. Ben was suitably impressed and clopped his two front feet up the first step. He could have easily fitted into the hotel, and I know that the landlady would not have minded – possibly because it meant their guest tally would have increased from two plus child plus dog to two plus child plus dog plus horse, but more probably because she is the sort of unphased landlady one could only wish for on a real holiday; like an adored teacher who turns a blind eye to rules. There are no breakfast deadlines, no 'No Dogs' signs, no 'No Walkers' signs, no 'No Smoking'

*Dreich – Scots for grey, dreary, bleak.

signs (anywhere), no 'No Children Under 3' signs in the bar. What we are receiving is an entirely personal, custom-designed service.

The hotel is run by a charming couple who moved here from the Midlands but never from the fifties. The hotel is empty, and gives every indication that guests are an exception rather than the norm.

'We had some other guests here with horses,' our landlady remembered fondly when she saw our saddle, packs, bridle and other paraphernalia filling up the entrance hall. She seemed wistful because they had been guests rather than because they had had horses. All the same, she never noticed the mess or the fact that Tess had made a beeline for the kitchen and Barnie for the bar.

'You can put all that in the guest lounge,' she said pointing to the saddlery. 'It'll not bother anyone there.'

The lounge is dark and made darker by decor and net curtains. It smells strongly of sick, and you get the feeling that the windows are locked tight by ancient paint. An overflowing ashtray sits beside the TV guide on the stained table. We follow more stairs and corridors whose walls are adorned with occasional paintings resembling chocolate box lids dug out from a nostalgic grandmother's attic hoard, or picked up for a quid in a car boot sale – there is one of a yacht sailing across a faded, dusty sea, and one of Eilean Donan Castle in what appears to be a bygone, misty age, except that several cars are parked nearby.

So to here, Room 21, Empty Hotel, Edzell. Home for now. Barnie is reclined on the bed, watching TV, drinking juice and eating raisins nonchalantly from a mug like an absent minded footy viewer with a packet of chips. Hand to mug to mouth. Hand to mug to mouth. As for Rob and I, we will be celebrating in the dining room tonight. Just us, a well positioned gas heater and fifty empty tables.

DUM SPIRO SPERO

Sunday 22 September

A Scottish town without a castle or abbey is like a fairy tale without a prince. Edzell may not be exotic, but it has the most stunning ruined castle which looks kind rather than fierce, aesthetic rather than practical. It is constructed of sandstone, and therefore coloured a mellow red, as though the evening sun perpetually strikes it. Behind, a green backdrop of a small wood and gentle hills offset the picture. Edzell Castle was the seat of the Lindsay family, or the 'lichtsome (carefree) Lindsays' as they were called. It is largely thanks to Sir David Lindsay, who acquired the estate in 1558, that the castle is anything but menacing. He was, apparently, a creative, passionate and enlightened man who carried out large scale afforestation on the estate and initiated the mining in Glen Esk. He also dedicated himself to his residence, and in particular his garden. The latter, a walled garden, was intended to provide stimulus to both the mind and the senses.

The walls are still remarkably intact. Each one is divided into compartments by stone columns and each compartment

183

displays a sculpture. On the east wall the theme for the sculptures is Planetary Deities, on the south wall it is the Liberal Arts, and on the west side it is the Cardinal Virtues. Not content with such work, Lindsay then decorated the walls with a series of round, carved niches, intended to display busts; recessed flower boxes; permanent nesting holes for aristocratic birds; and numerous other carved reliefs and decorations. These aren't walls but works of art.

In one corner of the garden is a wonderful stone summer house which has Wendy House proportions compared to the castle. This was the bolt hole in which peace could be found from Lindsay domesticity, but it was also the place where the garden could be enjoyed without actually being outside (a little like a pier on which you can enjoy the sea without being in a boat). How many 'balmy' Scottish evenings were spent in this beautiful but cold stone building – a hazard for new toddlers! Barnie was busy exploring the compact and geometric garden within the four walls. Although the garden was planned and built in 1604 and is recognised as one of Scotland's horticultural gems, the current one was planted after it had passed into State care in 1930. Excavations were carried out and the resulting garden is based on the findings. The result is low box hedges trimmed into ninety degree angles and sculptured to depict the thistle of Scotland, the rose of England and the fleur-de-lys of France.

Enclosing beds of yellow and red roses are more elaborate box hedges sculpted to incorporate the mottoes of the Lindsay family – ENDURE FORTE (endure firmly) and DUM SPIRO SPERO (while I breathe I hope). Lindsay must have been an eccentric of his time, designing such an elaborate garden while all around him feuded and thought mainly of survival and defence. Although the garden looks perfectly finished to the amateur eye, it wasn't fully completed when Lindsay died in 1610 'in extraordinary debt'.

For all its sophistication, serenity and beauty, Edzell Castle hides a darker secret. It is haunted by the White Lady, the wife of another Lindsay. One night she fell into a coma, was pronounced dead and was buried. One of the servants sneaked back to unearth the Lady and pinch her wedding ring. The Lady awoke and walked back to the Castle gates, asking to be let in. Everyone thought she was a ghost and fled in fright, leaving her at the gates. The night was cold, and the next morning the Lady really was found dead outside the gates to the Castle. DUM SPIRO SPERO – no family motto could be more appropriate.

Barnie thought the garden was planted entirely for his benefit. He rolled down the gentle grassy slopes and ran among the child-size box hedges. A walled garden is a perfect playpen for an amateur walker; but when box leaves were ingested, large holes appeared in the manicured hedges and he began his amateur scrambling up the crumbling walls, it was time to leave.

Near the current entrance to the castle, where the souvenir shop sells Edzell Castle tea towels, mugs, key rings and the usual array of Scottish history books, and the Edzell Castle blurb boasts that Mary Queen of Scots stayed here (where didn't she stay?), and the bored shopkeeper gave us little pink tickets and told us to keep Tess on a lead, Ben eyed us intently over the fence. Ben is sharing this field with cattle. The farmer looked worried when I turned him out yesterday and he galloped away across the field, sending the cattle running and the ground into tremors. But he is settled now with his bovine mates. I know that, from now on, we will have to seek fields for Ben to graze at night because there will be no open land on which to tether him. This week will need some planning.

Today has been a day off. So we visited the Castle... then went for a walk! Rob's car had been driven to Edzell by his parents, so we jumped into this and drove to neighbouring Glen Lethnot at a top speed of 40mph. Compared to 3mph, 40mph in a metal box was scary. Nevertheless, it was good to forget Barnie for a while as he sat in the back and looked askance at some plastic toys found on the floor. He will have to be weaned off hammers and rabbit droppings when we get home.

Glen Lethnot is another hidden delight west of Glen Esk. We ate a picnic near a small burn then walked uphill, avoiding any tracks and very aware that a horse was missing from the entourage. First I led the way, heading straight up, taking the shortest route possible regardless of the fact that it was the hardest route. Then Rob took over the lead and began zig-zagging uphill, taking longer but conserving himself better and perfectly illustrating the differences in our characters. We have, undoubtedly, complimented each other on this trip; like all relationships, we started the trip from very different points but have come together with a common goal, a common road.

I have a cavernous feeling of emptiness tonight having said farewell to Rob, and a strange and sudden sense of responsibility now that all links with 'home' have disappeared; all links with life 'as it should be'. Here we are, horse, dog, toddler and mother hen in Edzell. Before Rob entered our lives I was used to being on my own. But now…

I know too that cancer stripped away any self-confidence which remained after Barnie's father disappeared. Being faced with a weak spot in my body, and being made aware of my mortality for a second time, left me feeling like a raw wound that would weep at the slightest of knocks. After coming out of hospital I thought I should never face going out again. If someone had plonked me alone in Edzell ten months ago I would have wailed, fearing that the world was ready to 'get' me. Then I spoke to another lady who had had cancer and she felt the same … how much better I felt for knowing I wasn't alone.

Slowly, gradually, over time, the confidence has returned. My emotions are more raw, sensitive to feelings as a plant is sensitive to warmth or light. One minute the world is ripe and juicy, the next it can seem too overwhelming – rotten, beyond repair. The advantage to feeling the lows more acutely is that the highs are superb. And surely, given that my ability to cry is greater, so is my ability to laugh and to love?

In search of solace, I hit the hotel bar after Barnie had gone to bed this evening. There were around ten people lining the bar, the most I have seen in there. They all stopped talking when I walked in and took up my position between a fat lady with no neck and tourniquet rings which threatened to cut her fingers off, who was hunched over her brimming ashtray and pint, and a guy who gripped the bar rail yet swayed as gracefully as seaweed in a deep rock pool. Instinct inferred that he was looking at me, despite his glazed eyes being fixed on some distant land over my shoulder. I ordered a pint.

'A'right son?' the swaying wisp of seaweed slurred at me.

'I'm sorry?' I responded in my best English accent, looking at where his eyes were fixed over my shoulder, thinking there must have been a bloke standing there.

'Oahh,' came another slur. 'Thought you were a boy.'

I glared indignantly, but elicited no remorse. This being my sole interaction with my fellow drinkers, I took my drink out to the telephone and called my family. I haven't been mistaken for a boy since I was ten and, visiting Winchester Cathedral with my mother, was told to remove my hat; 'Boys don't wear hats in church,' I was told and decided then and there to grow my hair.

Our experiences in the bar last night were equally as memorable. Being our last night together, and in celebration of our arrival in Edzell, we decided on wine with our dinner. The bar lady showed us the wine list with a selection of around twenty. Rob ordered a bottle of Aussie red, but the bar lady came back empty handed.

'Sorry,' she said. 'We only have two wines in stock. A sweet white or a dry white.'

So we sat among our fifty empty tables, beside the gas heater, and drank dry white being flash chilled in a Moet ice bucket.

Last night's dinner is memorable for all sorts of reasons, though possibly not for its culinary expertise. But what this hotel lacks in stars, awards, guest numbers and standards, it makes up for in friendliness. There is something to be said for empty hotels and custom-designed service, in a place where profit must be an alien word.

You've Got to Go Through the Door

I had a dream that I was lying in a box lined with satiny material. It was cool and light and actually quite comfortable, but the place had no meaning. It was only when I woke that I realised the box had been a coffin.

I had such dreams as this time and again in the months after Christmas, after the operation, when I had told myself I should feel fine but my body was still sore and the abandoned psychological heap raised its 'C' shaped head. It is probably lucky that the disc on which I was writing then has been erased through some error. All that remains are the most striking thoughts, often the darkest, always the most determined, which cling to my memory the longest like beech leaves hanging on through the winter to be finally pushed aside by their successors in the spring.

In February, Rob, Barnie and I visited my sister in the Seychelles. Barnie was eight months old and was at that wonderful stage when he could sit but not crawl. So, while we swam and snorkelled, he sat under the shade of *a coconut palm with a handkerchief draped over his head, eating fistfuls of sand and blissfully ignorant of the coconuts thudding to the sand all around him. He watched his two aquatic cousins in awe, as their brown bodies bobbed in the brilliant blue ocean, and at night he slept directly under a fan and his little Scottish body sweated with the exertion of sleeping through humidity.*

It was a brilliant time of relaxation... until my groin began to ache and several lumpy nodes appeared. Then I felt one in my neck. Later, much later, I would be assured that they were 'harmless shotty nodes,' that they were 'side effects of having a number of lymph nodes removed,' that they were 'nothing to worry about'. But at the time I worried. The heat made them throb.

We flew home after two weeks, and I arrived back in Britain with a fluey, achy, diarrhoea virus. I felt terrible and will never know whether it was this virus, or worry, or depression, but the feeling persisted and persisted over the next few months. It took a gigantic effort simply to burrow out of my hole to start the day each morning, and usually my sole thought was to get back there as soon as possible. I struggled to care for Barnie, and had no energy for Ben. I decided I should sell him, but had no energy to do anything about this decision. The dreams continued.

All I could see was that before the operation I felt fine, but ever since I had felt lousy. My insides still felt as though they had been removed then put back in the wrong place and my body shaken hard. I still had stabbing pains round my bladder and bowel – and now I had shivery limbs and chronic exhaustion. Any semblance of rationality was *obliterated until all I saw was the fact that the doctors were united in some conspiracy against me. It was all their fault. I wished I had never had the operation.*

Somehow, remarkably, Rob stood by me. Our relationship moved on from platonic and this should have been the 'honeymoon' period – rosy, shining, exciting. Instead, Rob listened patiently to my loud abuse of doctors and replied with unwavering reassurance and endurance. Hardly a romantic start, but a pretty solid basis for understanding.

It wasn't just the cancer. I had vivid dreams of waking up to find Barnie had been snatched by his father, and others of hiding Barnie in the bathroom. Some mornings I honestly thought Barnie wouldn't be there. Other mornings I thought Rob wouldn't be there. Barnie's father had seriously undermined my confidence; the cancer had removed the rest. I tell you all this because, however much I tried to reason, however many mornings I woke with grand resolutions, I simply couldn't beat my body into action any more. Nor could I ignore the crazy mixed up emotions which, over the years, I had learnt to store in my British veneer. These emotions were too raw, too basic, too loud, too dangerous.

One morning I was outside with Ben. A massive flock of geese were feeding in a nearby seed field, filling their stomachs with pre-migratory food and the air with their chatter. There were already plentiful buds on the trees, and the daffodils in the dean were brilliant 'tossing their heads in sprightly dance'. I lifted Barnie on to my back and walked Tess around Ben's field. As usual I remembered ditties which my mother sung to us, and which I now sung to Barnie:

'It's too wide, you can't go round it,
It's too high, you can't go over it,
It's too low, you can't go under it,
You've got to go through the door...'

I had always thought of this as, well, a meaningless ditty. You would when you are young; now it suddenly made sense. I couldn't edge my way around or over or under this problem, ignoring something which tripped me up at every turn. I had to open the curtains to the smouldering heap which my dreams had been illustrating.

Let me take the cancer issue first. Imagine this: you are in a rambling old castle on top of a windswept moor at night, miles from anywhere, on your own. The castle is in utter darkness. Every window is sealed by shutters and there are no lights and no candles. You are in one of the upstairs rooms. The door is shut. You are now told there is a thirty per cent chance that there is a man in the room wielding a knife. You cannot see anything, only sense. That man has got you once before with his knife; you are still sore as a result. Now there is only a thirty per cent chance he is in the room. Nevertheless, given the setting, your past experiences of this man, your racing heart, the hair standing up on the back of your neck, I defy anyone to honestly say they could convince themselves the man wasn't there.

I was up there in the rambling house, with a thirty per cent chance that the cancer might strike again. Imagination isn't just a constructive thing, the gift of artists and authors and children – it is in all of us. It displays its darker side at times like this. Why else do people fear fun fair rides or spiders?

They fear the worst. Every time I feel unwell, have pains, or simply feel tired or down, the fear of the cancer returning surfaces. Accepting this is the first step. At the moment, and for the two years post-operation, I have check-ups at the hospital every three months. I am in good hands, though I haven't always recognised this. The doctors aren't united in conspiracy at all.

Which brings me on to the fact that the doctors have now saved my life twice. My incidence with the bee sting, and the doctors words – 'for a minute there it was touch and go' – come back to haunt me more frequently now. Every summer I watch bees with intrigue as they buzz around me, little killers. I am fascinated by them, fascinated by the effect they could have on me. Now I am fascinated by cancer and the frailty of life once more. If it wasn't for doctors I would be dead twice over. I cannot preach pure Luddite tendencies or bemoan technological advancements when I have benefited from such things not once but twice. My values have been challenged, and now they must be altered.

Next I have to accept that I have lost part of what it means to be a woman, that I no longer have a womb. Barren, spayed, they both have meaning now. Yet I have dreams of being pregnant and wonder with absurd irrationality whether there isn't just the smallest possibility of having a baby without a womb. How powerful the mind is. To accept this body wholeheartedly will take time, and time is itself an issue. I thought I would have no time, that I had to cram everything into now, aware of the tenuity of the future. But with each clear check-up, each healthy day, time gains perspective again and I can begin to solidify the blocks on which to build the future.

When I thought of my new body and the way it had been severed from the natural world, I remembered the coastal walk with fondness; my love and affinity for the world I walked with – the hills and streams, birds and flowers. I read Svn Edds, Entq Oavr and thought wistfully of undertaking another trip. The trouble was that I still had no energy.

My realisations had put a stop to the dreams and clarified things, yet changed nothing. I still struggled through the days but began to cling to the idea of a future trip. Despite the fact that I still felt I wasn't doing Ben justice, and wondered whether I should sell him, I planned the trip around him. Then Mr Mowbray called to say he had found a wicker basket saddle. And so, at the age of eleven months, before he could even walk, Barnie was strapped into this atop Ben and rode to the end of the drive and back. Virginia accompanied us on this epic five hundred yard trip, but both Ben and Barnie were unphased by the experience. Ben's ears flicked back and forth as he listened to the babbles from his jockey. Barnie grinned widely. It was a moment to treasure. The thought of walking in the hills with Barnie on Ben stirred something which had been dormant within me.

The seeds were sown. All I needed was some energy, and a little help in accepting the new person I had become. The person post-cancer, post-hysterectomy. It was at this time that I heard of Maggie's Centre.

Edzell

Monday 23 September. Day off.

We woke to a windless, sunny day and the sound of children playing in the playground down the road. It is a haunting sound which reverberates along time-tunnels until it seemed, this morning, as loud and familiar as it was twenty years ago and I was that child in the playground on a sunny morning's breaktime, drinking milk from little bottles and playing hopscotch or elastics. I felt and sensed chalk on the blackboard, bare knees, splintery wooden seats and the smell of sticking plaster, and wonderful Miss Pod with her grey bun and round spectacles. Then, a little older and more sure of myself, I remember locking all the loos in a row, crawling back underneath the last one and being caught and my friend, Mouse, and I being told we should have been born boys; or giggling at the naked bodies etched with a compass on to the back of the piano in the music room. They were fine works of art.

I felt sad and empty this morning, sensing all this and feeling 'homesick' with the absence of Rob as one is sometimes 'homesick' for childhood. Very soon it will be

Barnie going off with his own Miss Pod – only there won't be chalk or wooden seats or probably even music rooms (except virtual ones) in his school.

Barnie and I had a lonely breakfast, then set off with Tess to see Ben and measure his feet for the blacksmith. It is about a mile's walk to his field, through the edge of town and past the old mart with its ramshackle wooden pens. Corrugated iron has been ripped from the roof of the auction building, and weeds grow tall in the yards. A 'For Sale' sign is the only new thing – it reads 'Edzell Light Industrial Estate – 3.5 Acres.' By the time we return to Edzell some time in the future, the mart will be gone, the industrial estate will be complete and our hotel will probably have fallen prey to EC health and safety regulations.

Edzell has a forlorn air. It appears that here, situated between Highland and Lowland, the town is caught in a void. Although Edzell has a tartan shop and tweed warehouse, the hotel sells only two types of malt whisky. Although an elegant memorial arch frames the entrance road from the south, the picture within is neglected. I bought a postcard which illustrates the attractions of Edzell. First there is the memorial arch, built in 1888 in memory of the 13th Earl of Dalhousie and his Countess, who died a day apart. Then there is the intriguing 'Swingin' Brig' which isn't an upbeat dance step peculiar to the region, but a bridge over the River North Esk. And then there is the Panmure Arms Hotel – an enormous black and white hotel which takes up a large part of the High Street and yet is shut up, in limbo, waiting for a buyer and already looking the worse for its neglect.

Edzell High Street appears too big for its purpose, like a child swamped by an adult's coat.

I was finally told one reason why Edzell is so quiet. There used to be an American Airforce Base north east of here, but this has closed and taken with it 1,500 Edzell customers. Scott's newsagent will lose out badly – Edzell's population alone is hardly likely to read 1,000 *Sunday Sport*s.

I entered Scott's newsagent in search of blank tapes, a birthday card, a cake for Sophie (her birthday is tomorrow), and a picnic lunch. I could have come away with a selection of toys, sunglasses, fuse wire, condoms and stamps. Scott's newsagent is one of those wonderful rural shops which sells just about anything you need without a catalogue or order form in sight – home-made ginger cake and fudge being particular specialities. I like such shops for browsing and buying, and for discovering the time and whereabouts of yoga classes, when the chiropodist is visiting and who has a guinea pig or bicycle for sale. You can glean a lot from window notices. In the window of the coffee shop, I read about the Strathcarro Cancer Support Group. It is always reassuring to read about cancer support groups.

Back in the summer, when I was struggling with chronic exhaustion and coming to terms with the new me, I saw a notice in the doctor's waiting room for a Border's support group for women who had breast cancer. I knew I could benefit from talking to others who had had cancer, and this notice isolated me further. Then Rob came home with a leaflet about Maggie's Cancer Care Centre in Edinburgh. I plucked up courage, phoned them, and was soon driving to Edinburgh on a weekly basis. I say pluck up courage because

SMALL STEPS WITH PAWS AND HOOVES

I felt I had failed in not coming to terms with things on my own. How did we survive before the advent of support groups, psychologists and counsellors?

First, I suppose you got ill but rarely knew the name or implications of your condition. Cancer has become a Big Black Word through knowledge, let alone personal experience. Secondly, I can only guess that people talked more, amongst themselves, their communities, their families. And by talking, you probably came across someone who had a similar story to tell. Sharing common problems is reassuring and strengthening in itself. So, when I see such signs for support groups, it reminds me again that I am not alone. When you are diagnosed with something like cancer, you are simultaneously handed a bin liner of baggage which you can carry around until it becomes too heavy and you have to look inside and begin the process of sorting out the tangle within. Support groups help.

It has been a glorious late summer's day and the memory of an icy tent is already distant. Barnie and I have been in T-shirts since nine o'clock this morning, following our route around Edzell's attractions.

The Swingin' Brig is a suitably named suspension bridge over the River North Esk which runs alongside Edzell. On the other side, a path favoured by dog walkers weaves along the river bank then ends abruptly, presumably at the point of optimum dog relief where the owners can turn and walk back – job completed. We threw pebbles for Tess, then played a game of Pooh sticks and gazed into the clear water where a few fishes darted, oblivious to our presence. From

198

there, it was back past a bed of begonias planted to read 'Farewell to US Airforce Friends,' and on to the swings. I chatted conspiratorially into my dictaphone, watched by a woman with three children, while Barnie swung and stared as only a child can. He stared at the other children as they would stare at Big Ben. Other children are a novelty to him just now and so I have promised to enrol him in a playgroup when I get home.

When we got back to the hotel, a coach was parked outside the door and the landlady was frantically trying to feed its occupants. She had spent the day baking scones and frying chips for fifty elderly holidaymakers en route from Blackpool back to Aberdeen. Such coaches stop here regularly, the men and women flowing out of the bus and into the dining room, drinking tea, eating chips and scones, and flowing back into the bus without so much as a glance at the Swingin' Brig. Instead, Edzell will be rated on a tea scale ranging from Blackpool to Aberdeen.

This evening we visited Ben again and gave him his meagre handful of nuts, then returned to Edzell for tea in a small café. I feel as though I know Edzell. There is no car to jump into for the journeys around town, and we are already recognised in the grocers stores. But I am looking forward to leaving. More than one night in one place seems like an age.

Birthday Cake and Caterthuns

Tuesday 24 September

Today is another superb day and we emerged blinking from the dingy hotel, lured out by the silky threads of sun. Heavenly. Ben agreed. He skipped down the road from his field, his heavy hooves getting tangled in their own excitement, and was suitably restless while we loaded him up. Soph, who arrived late last night, looked nervous when I hoisted wee Barnie on to stamping Ben, assuring her that Ben would settle down.

We followed the deserted back streets of Edzell on to a yellow lane heading south west. From here, the drovers took a direct route to Kirriemuir then Blairgowrie, probably where the straight main road now runs, whereas we are sticking to lanes which run to the north. It doesn't matter that we aren't following directly in their footsteps. We have crossed the Grampians from north to south, marking the footprints and hoofprints of our stalwart predecessors, and sampling just a tiny taster of the problemsthey faced

– stubborn, restless and straying beasts, ice pillows, empty ram's horns, unwelcoming landlords, unavailable stances, bogs, boggy beds, monotonous diet, smothering cloud and weary bodies. Arriving here, in the fertile, kind lowland with its clear skies and comparative bustle, I can feel relief and achievement. The beasts are in good health. Apart from saddle sores (nappy rash), a large thumb and a dog with a ripped dew claw, we are in good fettle.

There is still distance to cover, and this lowland droving would have brought its own problems. In open Highland country the stances were free and open; as the drovers entered the Lowlands they had to pay for grazing. They paid 'grass mail' which varied with time and place but ranged from 6d (2½ pence) per score of cattle or one hundred sheep to 4s 6d (22½ pence) towards the end of the nineteenth century. In the first half of the nineteenth century, a drover might expect to be paid 3s or 4s a day, compared with 1s a day in the early eighteenth century. The total expense of a drover varied considerably; the cost of bringing a drove from Caithness to Carlisle (a remarkably short journey of twenty-eight days) in the early nineteenth century was reckoned to be 7s 6d per beast.

This was summer droving. If beasts were driven through winter or early spring, the added cost of hay would have been incurred. So grass mail was avoided when possible, meaning that the drovers sometimes pushed their cattle to cover larger distances and find free grazing. Other costs weren't so easy to avoid. Increasingly, as time went on and as the drovers pushed south, turnpike tolls, bridge tolls, river tolls – even payment for passing through someone's land or woodland, or passing through certain towns, was sometimes demanded. Then, when the drovers arrived at the trysts, they had to pay market dues. They clearly had to watch their pockets as well as their beasts.

We have no grass money or turnpikes, but we now have to contend with cars. The lanes we are following today are busier than I anticipated – modern day drove roads servicing farms, pubs, shops, small hamlets with consumer necessities. The verges are testament to this with their decorative crisp packets, coke cans and plastic bags. Tess weaves from one side of the lane to the other, sniffing out the discarded remnants of traveller's picnics and the decomposing remains of unlucky rabbits. She loves such trips as this for their ever changing smells, rather than the monotony of the same smells in the same garden or the same walk every day. The only thing she really complains about is the lack of a sheltered campervan in which to sleep at lunch time. But she is learning to find sheltered nooks, and how to make comfortable beds in the paraphernalia of saddle packs and Karrimats. She loves the fact that all meals are eaten on her level.

Barnie is delighted to have ample cars and tractors to salute. He sees a car coming before we do, indicating that he has by pointing and emitting loud 'Brmm, brmmm's then waving his arms frantically up and down in a request for them to slow down, as he has seen me doing. Then, when the car is up close, he gives them his very royal wave – hand held high and still, face impassive, followed by the slightest twitch of his wrist.

Ben is equally delighted to be back on reliable tarmac which can't steal a foot or trip him up, while also enjoying the company of other horses who race up to the fence to greet the travelling horse. This is horse and farming country – ploughed fields, new seeds being sown in precise rows, and round bales in sloping fields looking as though they are just meant to be rolled down hill in some rural equivalent to joy riding.

We walked only four miles today. I thought we had better break Soph slowly into this life, and I knew things would take longer again as we find a new routine. Soph has come from Leamington Spa, where she is temporarily living with her husband-to-be, a pilot. She is a keen walker, as long as the weather is reasonably fair and the pack isn't too heavy. Walking isn't really the issue here anyway, and packing, saddling up, caring for Barnie and Ben on the road are the most tiring things about this life. Aunt Soph is doing well. I have put her in charge of the kitchen, while I do battle with the tent. Unfortunately I haven't chosen the camping spot well, and the ground is like iron. The tent pegs buckle between hammer and ground.

We chose this spot more for its historical value than its comfort. We are camped beneath two Iron Age forts – the Brown and White Caterthuns. At first glimpse, from down here below the two hills, only the odd jutting tooth-like edge reveals anything other than a smooth sided hill. On closer inspection the flanks of the two hills are con toured into earth ditches and walls to create what were once sizeable and intricate settlements. How harmonious they are in this rolling landscape, like clay moulded into kind shapes by the potter's hand. Yet enduring too. Short of major catastrophes or too many interested visitor's feet they will surely last another three thousand years. We have walked up to the White Caterthun, so called because lichen covered boulders still cover the ramparts, giving a whitish appearance. The boulders must have been brought up the hill. The Brown Caterthun, half a mile away, is smothered with heather now brown in its winter garb. They certainly picked their spots, our Iron Age ancestors.

There was a post-sunny day haze this evening when we explored the rubble of boulders, but on a good day it would easily be possible to see the coast. To the north, the Grampians began their gradual escalation in height, almost blue looking in the haze. Up on this hill top, defence was the name of the game, but apparently at the cost of any natural shelter and readily accessible water. How did they transport water from the burn a mile down the hill?

The farm we are camped on is, not surprisingly, called Forthill. Ben is safely enclosed in a small field with the companionship of a Shetland who appears to have become fat on thin air, while we are camped a little way away beside a large stack of black baled silage. Soph has popped behind the bales and I am lighting the candles on her cake:

'Happy Birthday to you...'

Ginger cake on a tin plate, and cold tea topped with undissolved powdered milk. This is soon discarded in favour of Glenlivet. The sun is fast disappearing now. Tractors continue their dusky work, and below us the Tay Valley begins to twinkle like phosphorescence on a dark sea. Vehicle lights move soundlessly across the valley. We are looking down on our restless, illuminated society, and looked down upon by the pair of silent Caterthuns.

I wash Barnie in some heated water from a saucepan which trebles as dog bowl, occasional horse water bowl, and Barnie's basin – and dress him in only two layers. He doesn't need his Chuckroast tonight. I put him to bed while there is still a hint of light. He falls asleep easily tonight, unlike some nights when I have to hold him down until hysterical giggles cease and his eyes finally close.

I know that Soph is tired too but, as usual, we have plenty to talk about. Our friendship began when we travelled around Europe together aged seventeen, sleeping on beaches and station benches, eating pizzas in Pisa and sunbathing on deserted Alpine ski slopes. On one occasion the money ran out. It was a weekend and there was nothing we could do until Monday. We were on an Italian island and settled down on the stone pier for the night, watching the affluent yachties going about their business and dreaming of food – huge platefuls of it. Then, like a genie bearing a plateful of carbohydrate, a vision of culinary satisfaction, a solitary Italian came up and invited us on to his boat. It wasn't exactly a yacht, more a motorised cake tin, but he had food and that was the main thing. We boarded the boat, and were wined and dined by our genie and two male friends. They said they were off to Corsica the next day, did we want to go?

It is always with amazement that we remember this story – that we slept on their boat, the two of us squeezed on to one bunk, and woke up to the chug of the engine and the expanse of Mediterranean around us. The decision had clearly been one based on food; and, unfortunately, Soph spent the next twenty-four hours being violently sea sick, thus leaving me to fend off the advances of our genie. Despite the fact that he barely came up to my navel, I didn't have a lot of bargaining power. We were on their boat, out at sea. I battled tactfully for twenty-four hours and welcomed land as an albatross must after all its months at sea.

My friendship with Soph is based on many lows as well as the highs. In a way I think Soph is searching for time away from life too. Like me, her mother died of cancer some years ago. Then, when I was pregnant, her brother was diagnosed with cancer. He died within a year, followed, two weeks later, by their father. My respect for Soph is enormous, in the way she has coped, is still coping, with this. And here I can find someone who isn't afraid to mention cancer, who doesn't avoid the subject and isolate us both. We can talk of cancer and fear as others might talk of the weather. The time doesn't have to be 'right'. We can talk as we saddle up Ben, or cook pasta and broccoli jazzed up with a little more cream of asparagus soup. There is huge value in that.

Maggie's Centre

Women's magazines are full of articles such as 'Health and Happiness after Breast Cancer.' Health sections of bookshops hold titles by people who 'beat cancer' through their own powers, through positive thinking; and by people who have undergone horrendous cancer treatments but emerged smiling. You hear the same stories on the radio, of people who face cancer with frightening acceptance, courage and humour. The experience makes them appreciate life, reassess values and make grand resolutions. Cancer does all these things and more, but this picture of brave cancer sufferers isolated me further. I wasn't brave at all, and I hated myself more for not being brave when everyone else appeared to be. My role models weren't beautiful, skinny magazine models, but beautiful, brave cancer sufferers. I got on with my life because I had to, and I promised myself to make the most of every day as though it was my last, and I searched for reasons and answers, but never a day went by when I didn't think; 'Why me? This sort of thing happens to others. I'm scared. What if something happens to Barnie? What happens if the cancer comes back? What will happen to Barnie if I die?'

The old adage of 'You can't judge a book by its cover' has far deeper implications. All around me, every day, were people like myself who carried their own cross. Yet I saw them in the post office or supermarket, chatting, smiling, getting on with life. We all display a cover, and save the contents of the book for a select few.

It had been a fateful trip from the cottage with its acorn in Devon, to the Borders, Barnie, the cancer, meeting Rob in his surgery all those months ago when he felt the unborn Barnie kick. So it was probably fate which brought Rob home one day with a leaflet about Maggie's Centre Support*. Support groups are not for everyone. Many people cope with traumas on their own; others are reticent about joining support groups believing, as I had first done, that it is a sign of failure. It isn't failure – it is self-help. Some people are scathing about support groups: I had never contemplated them until now, when the strong desire to know that I wasn't alone in everything I felt and feared made me get behind the wheel and drive to Edinburgh. Only personal experience will tell whether they are for you or not.

When I first went to Maggie's Centre, the small building in the grounds of the Western General Hospital was alive with people. It was like the first day of a new school when everyone else appears to know each other. The difference was that we were all bonded by cancer.

---

*Maggie's Cancer Care Centre was founded by Maggie Keswick Jencks. She had cancer and felt that people like herself would benefit from a centre that would enable them to address all aspects of living with cancer, and inform them about the medical realities of their disease. Maggie's Centre now offers support groups, relaxation/visualisation workshops, foot massages (heavenly) and advice or information on every type and aspect of cancer.

Before I could join a support group, I saw the psychologist who oversees the group sessions. I wasn't entirely sure what I would say to him, or, indeed, he would say to me. But things just erupted. Barnie sat on the floor at my feet looking at Mum in amazement as out it all poured, everything that had happened, everything I feared. And do you know what he said? He said; 'Wow! That's a lot to cope with. It's OK to feel all these things, to feel afraid.' In the absence of platitudes, I knew why I was there.

Two weeks later I left Barnie in the hospital creche and joined the support group. There were around eight of us in the group, all young women with children and all, except for me, had had breast cancer. Some were undergoing radiotherapy or chemotherapy, while others had had no further treatment after mastectomies of various kinds, and others had finished all treatment. In the beginning all I could do was cry. The tissue box became an appendage, but I felt cushioned by the presence of people who understood, accepted and recognised the way I was feeling. As the weeks went by, I probably painted a fairly detailed picture of where I was 'at'. Each stroke added helped me see things more clearly, and the tears ceased. Then, as other people joined the group, I began to see myself in them.

Some people came before their operation or treatment, and appeared in the same state of numb shock that I remembered. Others came after, as I had done, at the time when the bag gets too heavy and you open it up, see the tangle and think 'help!'. Recognising myself in other people was as cathartic as sharing common thoughts and fears.

Our sessions weren't always morose. There were plenty of laughs; plenty of chat about breast reconstructions and whether soya ones would enable you to produce soya milk afterwards. It was always the tears-running-down-the-face real laughter of people who need it most, a bright moment relieving an almost tangible sadness. Laughter when you are down is like hurtling from an aeroplane without a parachute, seeing the ground race up towards you – then realising that you have wings and suddenly swooping up and gliding over the most stupendous sunbathed landscape; despair to euphoria in one beautiful moment, illustrating that the line between pain and pleasure is very frail.

Nor was our 'chat' just about cancer, but about the lives we led outside the room, because cancer has implications in every aspect of your life. Confidence is undermined, and this affects your relationships, your working life, your social life. At the same time, for those emerging at the other end of the tunnel, there was the sense of 'I'm going to do more things for myself now; look after myself.' It is true that you are useful to no one else unless you are healthy in body and mind, and Barnie needs me. Besides, I want to be around to see him undertake his own travels (hopefully he'll take me with him). So, while I was attending Maggie's Centre, I made a resolution to be kind to myself. I may not always like this body, but it is the only one I will have on this earth.

Perhaps, likewise, you cannot fight the road of fate. The quote at the front of this book takes me back to a time of undiluted peace – pre-Barnie, pregnant and pre-cancer. When I need to recreate peace, or when I get freaked out by the fate which led my life over the years between Barnie's conception and now, I remember the words:

> *God grant me the Serenity to accept the things I cannot change, Courage to change the things I can, and Wisdom to know the difference.*

I attended Maggie's Centre every week for five months, except for the three weeks it took to complete the drove trip. I stopped going after this because I felt there were people who needed my place more than me, and because I was commissioned to write this book and there just weren't enough hours in the week. We now have a graduation group which meets once a month. It was, undoubtedly, thanks to Maggie's Centre and everyone I met there that I began to find the new Spud, the one post-cancer. New, because you cannot ever go back to the person you were.

Droving at Last

Wednesday 25 September

Soph slept with her hat and coat on last night, inside her sleeping bag, and was still cold. Probably because of this, or the fact that Barnie was using his beaker as a vicious weapon at first light, Soph was up and lighting the stove before I had emerged from my sleeping bag. Her red hat bobbed outside the tent as though a dancing Smurf was below.

So we had porridge and air-chilled coffee for breakfast, and began to pack up for a long day. Pat, our kind farmer's wife, looked in after she had deposited her children on to the school bus. She took photos to prove to her family what a sight we were, then asked us in for coffee – hot coffee. Too much to resist.

The house was immaculate, or seemed that way from our perspective. An exercise bike was prominent in the kitchen (you eat your cream bun then leap on the bike to work it off again), and it wasn't long before Barnie had opened a door to reveal a cupboard full of toys, mainly tractors, chucked in here to be out of sight. This kept him amused while we scalded our mouths on coffee.

I remember a friend of mine who was incredulous that I set off to walk Britain's coast on my own saying that she wouldn't drive on her own at night. Trusting strengthens trust, and reaffirms the goodness which is still out there. People such as Pat have gone out of their way to make us welcome. Who knows? If you drive on your own you might come unstuck, but then you might also meet people as good as the others are evil.

We finally set off much later than intended. The lanes seem quieter today, as we follow the shoulder of the Hill of Menmuir past plentiful farms and the odd phone box or church which indicates the otherwise easily missable hamlets of Tigerton, Kirkton of Menmuir and Fern. This country seems so productive. Even the verges are green and lush, laced with the well worn paths and intricate tunnels of small beasts travelling from feeding ground to lair and back again, and at every opportunity Ben veers towards one verge or the other to take a quick but enormous mouthful of grass.

It is another gorgeous day. We have all caught the sun, and I am glad I packed a small pot of sun cream for Barnie along with his thermals. We have eaten blackberries from the hedgerows, and passed dried sticks and grasses to Barnie so that he can encourage Ben along from the saddle. Needless to say, this makes little impression on Ben's pace, and when we finally grind to a halt Soph gets behind him with a bushy twig. But Ben just wants to turn around and eat the twig. For him, it is a little like being hit on the bottom by a cream bun. Tasty vegetation is more helpful when carried along in front of him like the proverbial carrot.

Dear, one-horse-powered Ben. I have learnt to fit my pace around his, simply to make life easier. Sometimes, if there is a horse up ahead, or we are down hill with the wind behind, his pace is faster than mine and I have to keep up; most of the time his pace is slower. And as we walk along together, absorbing the sun and watching the county of Angus unravel into autumn, I chat into the dictaphone. The clip clop of Ben's hooves is as rhythmical as a metronome in the background, only interspersed by the odd 'Ooooo,' or 'Tessss,' or 'Brmmm,' from Barnie.

Plonked on this rural landscape, between ancient standing stones and the rolling hills, is Noranside Prison. We are having lunch on their boundary fence, in a small, grassy lay-by. Nearby, a group of cheery inmates are harvesting a field of 75,000 onions. They called out to offer us some, perhaps imagining strings of onions hanging from the withers of Ben rather than from the handlebars of a bicycle. The other end of the field was full of carrots and probably plenty of Peter Rabbits.

Our lunch spot is perfect. Ben is tied to a gate and has ample grass within reach. He has had his fill, and now stands with his head hanging over the gate to where we are. His bottom lip is wobbling, one back leg is resting, and his tail swishes involuntarily at flies. His stance is one of pure relaxation. Barnie also looks pretty relaxed. He too has had his fill, and is asleep on a Karrimat rolled out in the shade, in his T-shirt and sun hat, and with his hands acting as a cushion under his head. This is a time of complete peace and reflection. A twisted elder branch is my focal point, stuck on to the blue sky and textured and shadowed by the sun. The leaves are really starting to brown now and I can't help thinking about the proximity of the prison, and the inmates of so many prisons who must crave the light of day and evidence of the seasons. It makes me think of the vast prison that I walked past on the Isle of Sheppey. Then, as now, I am almost guilty of the freedom I have. There could be no greater juxtaposition – life on the road to life in a cell.

From Noranside it was only four miles to Memus, where we are staying tonight. When I did a recce trip of this area, looking for places to leave caches of goodies, I came around the corner into the village of Memus and there was The Drovers Inn. It was too significant to overlook and I was soon chatting to Jim the proprietor and telling him about the forthcoming trip. By the time I left he had offered us a field for Ben and a roof for the night.

From our twentieth-century perspective it would seem natural that the drovers made the most of any inns they came across, especially once they had reached this more populated lowland country. But the reverse was true. Pre-nineteenth-century Highland inns were undesirable places. They were wayside cottages in which the traveller could neither 'eat or sleep with comfort,' but in which there was always plentiful illicitly distilled spirit. The eighteenth-century government unsuccessfully tried to rectify the absence of decent inns: Kinghouse, on Rannoch Moor, was on a busy droving route and in an effort to keep this inn open the innkeeper sat rent free and was paid a government grant. Nevertheless, it was described in 1802 as having 'more the appearance of a hog stye than an inn.' In 1803, Dorothy Wordsworth made a tour of Scotland and was more eloquent but no more complimentary in describing Kinghouse as 'a wretched place – as dirty as a house after a sale on a rainy day.'

As the nineteenth century wore on, and the routes of the drovers became more defined and restricted, inns became more commonly used by them. But droving was beginning to decline by this time, and those who continued to drove often preferred to sleep out. Theirs was a tradition as well as a life. However, the thought of a shower and not having to put up the tent was enough for us. Little did we know we would actually be droving at The Drovers. What a caper when we arrived!

There is a small field behind the pub in which live Fiona and Shuna, two young, hand-reared Highland cattle who had never left their field – nor seen a horse. 'Oh, stick Ben out in there with them,' Jim said casually. By this time the pair had retreated to the other end of the field where they cowered behind a thorny bush, but I did as Jim suggested. That was it. Fiona and Shuna were out of there, terrified. They leapt *at,* rather than over, the wire fence, into the vegetable garden, then ploughed through another wire fence and finally, third time lucky, made a clean jump off the lane and into a field of sprouting wheat. Ben stood, ears pricked at the commotion, looking more than a little incredulous. He is usually so friendly with cattle that I'm sure he thinks his hooves are cloven. You can imagine that this exit left him rather confused and put out.

So, as the sun went down, we found ourselves walking west into it following a pair of short, shaggy brown Highland cattle who stuck to each other like magnets. Fiona and Shuna are supposed to be tame enough for Jim to show them next year, but I can't picture them in the show ring, only out of one. They calmed down as we walked them to a neighbouring farm for the night, Barnie staring transfixed from my back. It is dark now and Ben is sweating and galloping around the small field. I thought, at first, he was looking for mates. Then a series of rumbling moans made him quiver and start all over again. There is a venison farm not far from here, and the stags are well into their rut. It is an alien sound for anyone; especially for an urban, Irish, agoraphobic horse with a security problem.

I've fed Barnie fish fingers, carrots and chips in the pub, washed him in the basin, and put him into his sleeping bag in the annex where we are sleeping. There are no beds, but we have space and a temperamental shower. Unfortunately, I didn't have time to use the latter before we were summoned to join Jim for dinner. I spruced myself a little and was quite pleased with the result – the same wacky leggings and walking boots, but a clean T-shirt. Jim wasn't so impressed.

'What a scruff!' he declared.

Jim is one of those people you feel you have known for years, and vice versa. So I shouldn't have been put out by his declaration. But I was. The audacity! If he had spent almost three weeks living on and in the contents of one saddle pack, and had cared for a dog, horse and young child, I don't suppose his tweeds would look perfect.

Besides, there was no room to pack the 'because you never know who you might meet' skirt, and a kilt was never an option. So I have scraped my hair back into a new bunch, and shunned the alternative of filthy tracksuit bums and bare feet. Oh well. Never mind the attire – food is foremost in my mind.

Camped on a Field of Magic Mushrooms

Thursday 26 September

The ram's horn never ran dry last night. The beasts were safely enclosed, the bairn was asleep (monitored by the baby alarm which Rob had mistakenly left with us), and we celebrated the droving life until even the stags had ceased their raucous display of courtship. We are suffering the consequences. Everything today is slow, and departure is being delayed by the blacksmith putting new and hefty shoes on Ben. It may seem inconceivable, but the drovers actually shod their cattle because new, gravelled roads were hard on the cattle's feet too.

General Wade is a name synonymous with many of the Highland roads. He built nearly 250 miles of military roads in the Highlands between 1723 and 1740, and set Highland road building in motion. Though a large proportion of these avoided the open, remote country used by the drovers, others were constructed on their exact routes. As time went on, more and more of the drovers' roads were upgraded and gravelled and the drovers resorted to shoeing their beasts.

The shoeing of working cattle has been dated back to Roman times, though it is unclear whether this practice continued regularly through the centuries that followed. It is known that cattle were shod in England in the seventeenth century, and even as late as the beginning of this century, and that Welsh drovers also shod their cattle on their way to English markets. It was clearly not such a barmy idea as we might think. The Highlander's cattle started their journeys from the north without shoes, but once they hit gravelled roads they sought out smiths. They had to know where to find a good smith, and reputations grew. It was then a matter of turning each beast over to attach the eight, comma shaped shoes, called 'cues'. Each foot had a shoe on the outside of each hoof, where the foot wore down the most. They were thin shoes nailed on with three to five nails, and turned down on the top edge to give more grip on the roads. It must have been some operation to shoe a drove of a thousand beasts.

As the droves moved south, and often on towards markets in England, the shoes had to be replaced at intervals, either at local smiddies or with spare shoes carried by the drovers. And it wasn't just cattle which were shod. Other beasts driven from pasture to market over the centuries include pigs, sheep, geese, turkeys and donkeys! These were mainly found travelling the countryside of England and Wales; trails of thousands of poultry flocking to the main markets of London and Nottingham would have been some sight. Geese were driven to a small extent in Scotland, and these were 'shod' by smearing their feet with pitch and coating them with sand!

Donkeys were mainly driven from England back to Ireland by drovers who had brought cattle over to English markets. Donkeys were much sought after in Ireland for carrying turf, creels, milk and other goods: while back at home, they were in hot demand for holiday rides on Hampstead Heath, and beach rides in Brighton and Margate. There, I have found a link between the good old British seaside that I know and love, and the life and work of the drovers!

With Ben shod, Barnie decided he was tired, so I posted him back into his sleeping bag and we had a peaceful read in the sunshine before the off. By the time we left, the first pub goers were arriving. A group of men and women watched us with interest, and asked about the trip. When we told them we were raising money for Maggie's Centre, one guy told us that he had had cancer in his eye. 'But I've passed the five year hurdle now,' he said with a smile. If you get through five years post-cancer without a recurrence, then you are considered cured.

The group dipped into their purses and set us on our way with a little more weight. With Barnie anointed in more sun cream, we meandered along the lanes heading westwards, which rose and fell to negotiate the Rivers South Esk and then Prosen and passed through beautiful beech woodland enshrouding Cortachy Castle. If the trees had ears, they would have heard Soph and I deep in conversation – we talked of Soph's wedding plans, of the perfect place to live (warm weather, hills, sea). We talked of mutual friends, of travel and shared experiences (those blasted cockerels and dogs of Laos whose combined cacophony woke us at 5 a.m. without fail – some holiday), and we talked of grief, cancer and fear – cheery subjects for such a beautiful day. BT got one thing right; 'It's good to talk'… 'and easy to talk while walking' would be my addition.

If our lives are fast, then our thoughts are fast and furious. Talking, thinking – both are possible when walking. You cannot think faster than the rhythm of your footsteps (believe me, I've had several thousand miles of practice), which is presumably why 'power walking' came into existence – to cater for the relentlessly cascading thoughts of a stressed out executive. It is easy to see why pilgrims walk to re-gather the scattered particles of themselves – spiritually, religiously or otherwise. Some people need mountains to feel whole, some people won't venture out without make-up; putting one foot in front of the other is my sustenance.

I hit a problem, post-operatively, when I simply couldn't walk. I sat still for too long, and felt ill as a result. It took a while before I was strong enough to walk far enough, or pain-free enough. Rediscovering my ability to walk, my strength to walk, has been the most important thing. Some people have called it running away, and, if I'm honest, this trip was initially an attempt to put a full stop to the events of the last two years; but that could never happen. By walking away I haven't solved anything, but I am regaining an equilibrium which has been blatantly missing.

Yesterday we covered ten miles, and Barnie was in the saddle for the entire time, happy as a horse with meadow hay. Today we have only covered five and a half miles before reaching this perfect camping spot thanks to a kind farmer who has potential to diversify his agricultural enterprise – 'PYO Magic Mushrooms'. Ben has fourteen acres of wacky pasture to explore and fresh water from a burn clogged with watercress. I wonder if horses and cattle sometimes eat the hallucinogenic mushrooms? If Ben gets much more laid back we'll have to carry him. Barnie too has an expanse of pasture to run around in, but I'm keeping a close eye on him to make sure he doesn't eat a mushroom and go on some colourful trip without me.

The tent is up and the sleeping bags laid out along with Barnie's pyjamas and penguin. Soph is at the stove, stirring a bubbling brew, while I feed Tess and mix powdered milk for Barnie. Witnessing this rural domesticity is a stand of heraldic beech trees crowning the horizon, silhouetted black against the fading day and motionless in the still evening. Trees have definitely been our guardians today.

The Decline of Droving

Friday 27 September

Last night we had a room with a view at the cost of level land. I slept at the bottom of the heap with my nose pressed against canvas drenched with bodily condensation, and woke repeatedly with Barnie wedging me against the tent with Soph close behind. Tess just ensures that she is permanently glued to somebody, and moves as you move away from her, stuck to bodily warmth like an efficient parasite. All very cosy.

It is a soupy day today with low cloud sitting on the country, decapitating trees and making everything damp. Packed up at last, we walked back along the wooded lane to a crossroads marked by a red phone box – a K6 phone box, according to Soph, whose husband-to-be, Robert, is a phone box spotter. 'K6 are the most common red phone boxes. Around 63,000 of them were built in the 1950s. They put public phones on the map,' Soph assured me. 'You'll know it's a K6 and not a K2 by the crown above the door. Now a K2 is a spotter's delight,' Soph laughed. 'You'll have to talk to Robert about them.' Robert warms to his subject on the phone.

'And people think a red phone box is just a red phone box! I ask you...' (*And* he's being serious.)

'You'll know it's a K6 because they have an embossed crown above the door, as opposed to the K2 which has a crown made up of little holes. If you find a K2 you're lucky.

'But to go back to the beginning. First there was the K1. There's only one of them left now, in Bembridge on the Isle of Wight. The mecca for phone box spotters. One day I'll get there.' (Help! He's into his stride and there's no stopping him.)

'The K4 was brilliant. It included a twenty-four hour post office, but the stamp machine was pretty noisy when you were on the phone. It had a letter box included. There are only two of them left in the country.

'Then, of course, the K6 appeared all over the country. You'll know its a K6 because of the crown, and if you look on the back, two inches above the ground, you'll see an oval plate naming the foundry. Then there are the cable inlet points...'

My mind wandered while Robert continued with spotter's enthusiasm, as an art lover might talk of a painting or a twitcher might talk of a rare feathered visitor, and I was only left wondering whether the poor unsuspecting Soph was off to the Isle of Wight for her honeymoon.*

We wandered through more woodland and along steep little lanes which soon took the flight out of Ben's hooves until I seemed to be pulling him along, taking small steps

---

*Soph is since married. It was a grand wedding and I can assure the reader that she wasn't taken phone box spotting to the Isle of Wight for her honeymoon.

with heavy hooves. While Barnie is thriving on this life, and seems to be calmed by the clip clop of the hooves beneath him, Ben is encouraged on only by the sight of lush verges or the promise of an imminent rest. His temperament is purely pony. A group of shooters watched our progress, their loyal yellow labradors panting heavily by their sides, but apart from that the lanes were empty. Sheep and cattle grazed obliviously either side of us, making the most of autumn grazing before they are brought inside for the winter.

The drovers would have also been thinking about winter and pressing ahead now, aware that their costs were creeping up, grazing was increasingly scarce, their beasts were getting weary, and the last tryst of the year was imminent. Crieff was the first large tryst to be formed. Its arrival followed improved relations between England and Scotland and the subsequent abolishment of all export and import duties between the two in 1669. Crieff was centrally located and trading started here in 1672. By 1723, 30,000 cattle were sold here at the October tryst. This took place in the second week of the month, forcing the drovers to be rid of their beasts, whatever the cost, rather than face the added journey of moving further south to find another autumn market. Some drovers were hired by English buyers to drive the beasts on into England, where they stayed through autumn and early winter and helped smear the sheep in tar and butter – an eighteenth century practice which was considered essential for keeping the sheep warm and free of parasites!

Crieff tryst was soon eclipsed by Falkirk tryst further south, which meant a little more travelling from the

Highlands but a little less travelling for the English buyers. At its peak, in the early nineteenth century, Falkirk tryst was held three times a year – August, September and October. During this time a staggering 150,000 cattle were reported as sold annually at Falkirk. What a sight it must have been, as Gaelic mingled with Yorkshire dialect, Western Islanders haggled with Cumbrian folk, strong Aberdeenshire accents struck deals with Borderers or Northumbrians. There were no auctioneers, so buyers bargained directly with sellers and there would have been many a wry word and passion spent among the hundreds attending; all the time, beasts and dogs and ponies looked on, or mingled and fought with each other, locking horns or teeth, and adding their own noises to the confusion. For the several days of the tryst, fires burnt bright to keep the men warm and fed, and ballad singers, fiddlers and beggars added the finishing touches to what must surely have been a brilliant spectacle.

Unfortunately, droving was set to decline rapidly from around 1860. The events which caused it may have been foreseeable to some, but they all came together in a hard hitting way, leaving the drovers redundant. The increase of tolls for roads, stances and wayside grazing grew during the eighteenth century, as did the amount of enclosed land and land set aside for sporting ventures. Dry stone dykes forced the drovers to keep to certain routes, while other routes were barred by lack of grazing, and increased arable land meant that landowners were vigilant. Then came the humble turnip, which, along with rotations and the improvement of pasture, helped destroy the droving trade.

Until now, Highland farmers couldn't overwinter or fatten cattle, which is why the drovers relieved them of their beasts in the autumn. But the turnip was brilliant winter feed, and now the farmers could hang on to their beasts and sell when the price was right – whatever the time of year.

The final insult came to the droving trade with the arrival of the steam engine. In about 1830 the first cattle were transported south on steam ships – setting sail from Banff or Wick or Aberdeen and arriving in London almost as fat and heavy as they were when they left. Then came the railways, which meant that buyers could delve deep into the Highlands, purchase stock direct from graziers, and bring them south by train. It is said that some old drovers insisted on accompanying their beasts on the train. And so, with this last blow, the closing years of the nineteenth century saw the last flicker of flame extinguished from the drovers' fire, leaving only the well-fertilised stances and the hoofprints of hundreds of beasts which once carried themselves across miles of Highland terrain to market.

Our original aim was to reach Crieff, but the contagious roads are hogging more and more country now and busy roads are not an option. Blairgowrie is probably as far as we will get by Monday, the day Virginia is set to pick us up. We are in the company of a couple more Highland cattle tonight, but they bear no resemblance to Fiona and Shuna in temperament and were positively delighted to welcome Ben over the fence. This is Peel Farm, a tourist farm with a Clydesdale horse, cattle, chickens, guinea pigs, and a pet rabbit which runs around the farmyard at its peril – Tess' equivalent to meals on wheels. Best of all it has a coffee shop selling all kinds of crafts and delicious home-made scones. Frances, our host, could not be more generous.

It is amazing how far south we feel now; the farms passed us more quickly this afternoon as we walked the final five miles of the day, passing through Kirkton of Kingoldrum then Bridgend of Lintrathen, and the lanes run straighter, unhampered by hills. We followed the shore of Loch of Lintrathen for the last mile, watching small motionless boats adorned with expectant fishermen sit on the smooth surface like patient predatory insects.

A row of smart, clean cars were parked near the loch, waiting for their fishermen owners. This beautiful loch, with its wooded shores, is a water supply for towns in Angus and Perthshire. How well-used it is compared to the secret lochs of further north, where otters, deer, grouse and ptarmigan are the main customers. The road was busier, and one car pulled up to ask the inevitable questions; Where to? Where from? How long? Then; 'Is this your holiday? Do you always take holidays like this?'

This isn't quite the average lie-in-the-sun-and-read-a-book holiday (which right now sounds like heaven), but it is a walking holiday and the only way we can walk any distance with Barnie is if we have Ben to carry him. It also seems that you become public property when you do a trip like this, and people lose inhibitions and ask any manner of questions. They also go out of their way to donate money.

One miserable, drizzly night, when Rob and I were camped in Cow Pat Field near Ballater, we were settled down in our sleeping bags by 9 p.m. when a voice suddenly came from outside the tent; 'Are you the couple following the drove roads?'

We replied we were, and made a vague attempt to find a torch, when a hand appeared under the tent flap and deposited a ten pound note.

'Who are you?' we asked.

'Gillian,' came the mysterious reply. The man then disappeared.

We shall never know who found us that dreary night in the middle of nowhere. But if you're out there, thank you!

Danger and Opportunity

Saturday 28 September

Forget shelter, water and not camping under trees or near main roads, Camping Rule Number One should be; 'Never camp below roosting cockerels.' Our roosters woke us at six this morning, four of them (I identified the different crows, including the pathetic one with a sore throat) and set off a series of events.

Barnie crawled out of his sleeping bag, helped himself to his waiting milk, then bit Tess. Tess growled, and I growled back at the pair of them from within my sleeping bag. Then Barnie howled, so I dressed him and packed him outside where he is happiest. Tess snuggled into Barnie's sleeping bag, and peace resumed. By the time we sat down to eat porridge, the cockerels, tired out from their crowing, were dozing again. A lunch menu of cockerel was considered, but declined – mainly because Rob arrived late last night for our final weekend and brought supplies with him. It is amazing that we have only passed one small and very spartan shop since Edzell.

We are quite an entourage today, now that Rob is with us, pushing his bike so that he can cycle back to his car later. Everyone is striding out. It never fails to amaze me how quickly you can cover the country on foot, linking the places together without leaving the ground. Being driven in a car is often like taking the London underground in that you never trace routes. You might sit on the tube for half an hour little knowing that you are only travelling a mile, and it would be quicker to walk. I have certainly done that – whereas now I will remember every step of this route; each turning which brings a new view, each farm which triggers a thought, each doggy or fishy weathervane which whirls or is still, each wayside bush which acts as loo... and each time I am caught by a passing motorist. Perhaps not very important information in the scale of things, but you realise just how small Britain is.

At Bridge of Craigisla we turned an abrupt left on to a busier brown road, then, after a mile, back on to this quiet yellow road just north of the Hill of Alyth. The countryside has changed again from productive grass and arable to more open pasture, moorland almost, which appears devoid of any livestock. There is suddenly an abandoned air, exaggerated by the dreariness of the day which sweeps in an unbroken grey arc from thumb-tip to thumb-tip above and beside us. There are no clouds and no patches of sky, just as there are no stock in the fields or cars on the lane. We are suddenly here all alone, surrounded only by standing stones and imperceptible settlements and field systems of an unimaginable age.

I am watching Ben, Soph, Barnie and Rob up ahead. What a sight they make. Did I create this? My mind flicks back to a time when I dreamt of this trip; and a time when any life post-cancer was virtually incomprehensible. I remember learning that the Chinese have two ideograms for the word 'crisis'* one means danger and the other opportunity. I hunted desperately for this promised opportunity as one might search for a mate when everyone around you is paired up. Neither search is fruitful. My opportunity is here, in front of me now; the opportunity to travel and experience and live and love. It is a great feeling to be part of something challenging and rewarding, and I sense that both Rob and Soph feel that now too, as the end nears and we are all together. Very soon, the memories of cold nights and endless pasta will be looked back upon as something to cherish – possibly. This deserted, open moorland between Bamff wood and Heatheryhaugh is the peace before the bustle, the empty before the full, the silence before the noise of returning to the cottage in the Scottish Borders which I have been calling home.

The lane is hedged with heather and gorse, but no fence, and sheep roam with a friendly Highland pony. Then, from Heatheryhaugh, the farms come regularly again as we drop down into Glen Ericht. The cottages are constructed of mellow red sandstone, and the hedgerows are adorned with blackberries, sloes, hazelnuts and conkers. Autumn, a time of gathering.

A pair of Clydesdale foals have just been turned out in a field, watched by a family gathering. Ben is frightened of the foals and skitters past. He is finding his downhill momentum

*There are actually three parts to the Chinese word 'crisis' (quoted above). The first character means 'danger'; the second has two parts - a) 'crucial point' and b) 'opportunity'.

and Barnie, who once swayed out of unison with his steed, now holds on to the strap with confidence and sways with him from side to side. Then, for some reason, Ben starts to whinny. He blasts the mouthpiece of the dictaphone, and Barnie, whose bottom lip once quivered whenever Ben whinnied, remains unperturbed.

Rob and Soph catch up as we see the white building of the Bridge of Cally Hotel. It is on the main road running through wooded Glen Ardle, and we have passed it so many times on recce trips to the north. 'Is this the end of the walk?' Rob asks. It signifies the end, though we will walk on to Blairgowrie tomorrow. But the end doesn't really mean anything. There will be no welcome or festivities, except in our own hearts and minds, because achievements don't need an ending. They can go on in different places with different maps and varying themes. This journey has just been part of the whole journey, and, like the whole journey, not all parts are pleasurable; but each twist and turn helps shape the unworked stone we are given at birth. Journeys like this aren't really necessary. Every one of us is journeying right now, though often we can be blind to the scenery and fellow travellers.

I remember stopping at a service station one time when I was driving from Scotland to Wiltshire with Barnie and Tess. The journey is a long one, and I was in a hurry to give Barnie his lunch, let him waggle his legs, squeeze Tess, then get going. I went into the ladies and laid Barnie on the floor outside the loo.

'Do you want me to hold him for you?' the young cleaning lady asked. I brushed her aside with a 'thank you but no thank you', but when I came out of the loo she was cooing at Barnie. 'He's beautiful,' she said.

I asked her if she had any of her own. 'I can't have children,' she told me. 'But we're trying for adoption right now. It's a long slow process.'

So we entered a long conversation about adoption, and I thought; 'I deprived this lady of holding Barnie because I was in a hurry, and I almost missed out on this rare meeting.' I often wonder how this lady is doing, and remember her whenever I am in a hurry. An opportunity almost lost.

We are camped in the garden of Bridge of Cally Hotel, tucked away in the damp and vegetative corner, home to slugs and undesirable slimy creepy crawlies; out of sight of a group of wedding guests dressed in their finery and sipping champagne from crystal flutes. We are sipping champagne from our tin mugs. The coffee stains are coming away from the tin and float on the bubbles along with pieces of grass and goodness knows what else. It tastes just fine in the semi-dark.

I feel elated, but absolutely exhausted. I am going to sleep and sleep when we get home. The thought of a cot for Barnie and a field for Ben, and a bath and bed. Then I can lay down the juggling balls of motherhood and groom and sleep the sleep of the sleep-deprived. I leave Rob and Soph nattering in the hotel bar and join Tess and Barnie in the tent. In the background, the little burn chats incessantly and will either make me sleep well or make me want to pee all night. Ohhh... for no tent zips, a bed and a sheltered loo.

An Unceremonious Ending

Sunday 29 September

It isn't just humans who have forgotten how to hunt, and now rely on quick, fast food and service. Ben's field last night had a beautiful burn at the bottom of a steep embankment, but when I led him down to it he snorted at the water tumbling over the boulders. It is like preferring an apple from a supermarket shelf to an apple from a tree; urban Ben the pavement horse prefers a water trough to the clear water of nature's tap. He has been so calm today, possibly because I have, and I feel such enormous love for the whole family. Rob picked up his car last night and we drove Soph to Perth station this morning. We returned, retrieved Ben, packed him up, and began the final four miles to West Gormack – a farming hamlet west of Blairgowrie which I have identified as a good spot for Virginia to find us tomorrow.

The path up from Bridge of Cally took us through a corner of deciduous woodland with low hanging birch branches. Barnie sees the branches coming now. He screws his eyes shut, and turns his head away with a rascally smile on his face. Watching out for such wicked branches is one of his games. He laughs delightedly, and bangs the Karrimats each side of the saddle as though drumming on one of those vast skewbald horses at the Trooping of the Colour.

Underfoot, the path was boggy, and got more so when we emerged from the wood on to Cochrage Muir – a plateau of moorland avoided by all modern roads, but negotiable on a dead straight track which began as a Roman road, was possibly a drove road, and certainly a military road. It would have been a hostile moor for the Romans to settle on, but settlements and field systems and the intricate earthworks of Buzzart Dikes indicate that they spent some time here, wrapping their togas tight against the damp and their possessions against wolves and natives. It must have been such a far cry from their own sunny country. It isn't surprising that they didn't stop long in Scotland.

The moor can have changed little since the Romans were here. It is carpeted in low heather, and the 'road' is only visible because of rubbly stones either side of the single file track. A couple of deer disappeared into the murk, and at one point a rough bridge had all but collapsed. We removed Barnie while Ben negotiated the hazard, but Ben sniffed at my concern and managed such obstacles easily. In fact, the path was harder for Rob with his bike than for Ben. A point for Ben.

The 'road' rose and fell away in front of us for two miles, and all around the horizon was flat, abruptly cut off where brown heather met ashen sky. Drizzle threatened many times, and I willed it to stay off until we had reached West Gormack and the tent was up – then, I told myself, it could do what it wanted. Rain, snow, gales. Tomorrow we will be in four solid walls, with cobwebs and curtains and carpeted floors. The glow induced by exercise and fresh air is engrained in me now, and I can look forward to such luxuries as clean hands.

By the time we reached the first house at the end of the dead end road, the drizzle was falling, light as dew at first, but meaning business. Middleton House looked spooky. Its windows were as dark and bottomless as a Highland loch, and there were shot holes in some. It didn't take long to discover that this wasn't Dick's place, the guy we had been told about by Frances from Peel Farm. We found Dick a little further on, over the Lornty Burn at West Gormack Farm.

Dick had been out feeding the cattle. He was driving an old tractor and had a woolly hat pulled firmly over his ears, from beneath which came a broad and experienced grin which put me at ease. For some reason, I felt an immediate warm bond with Dick. He made me feel comfortable, like a well-loved home full of comfy chairs, worn cushions, content dogs and interesting nicknacks.

'Of course you can stop here the night,' Dick said. 'The boss isn't here just now, but he won't mind. You can put your horse in that field by the burn, and camp anywhere around here that you want.'

We began unloading Ben and putting up the tent, hurrying to get everything under cover before the rain really began. If it wasn't for Rob, and now Dick, I would have felt depressed by the grey, damp ending on offer.

Rob pedalled back to his car in the rain, and left Barnie and I exploring the barns next to the tent. Barnie was in heaven, toddling around and around the real tractors, falling every now and again on to the dusty floor, but impressing us both with his balance which had been minimal at the start of the walk. How much a child learns in the space of three weeks! It was gloomy in the dark in the barns, and I could see the lights from Dick and his wife's cottage a little way along the road. Then, from out of the gloom came Dick's tractor again. He pulled up alongside and opened his door.

Dick was a bit of a phenomenon. In 1985 he was diagnosed with cancer and told that he had two years maximum to live. Twelve years later, after a heart by-pass and badly in need of a hip replacement, Dick was healthy and active. Sadly he has now passed away but during his illness he was the focus of media attention because of his extraordinary defiance of illness. He became an active fund-raiser for the hospital which treated him. But you wouldn't guess any of this when you saw him sitting cheerily in his tractor, entirely at one with life on the land. Is the fact that he lived so long due to his earthy philosophy of 'getting on with life'; believing so strongly in himself that cancer cells simply couldn't survive? He was as clear an example of such shining optimism that he put shame to my worries and musings. Fear is so tiring that it *must* deplete your body's energy stores. Yet it is easy to be theoretical, and so much harder to stifle imagination and really convince yourself that optimism and getting on is the best alternative. It is those differences between us, after all, that makes each one of us unique.

Perhaps age has something to do with it too? When you are sixty or seventy you expect to have more ailments than when you are thirty; and when you are thirty and have had cancer you lose all confidence in your body and wonder; 'If I'm like this now, what will I be like when I'm sixty? Will my body even last that long?' Perhaps, at sixty, you accept ailments more easily, relaxing into the role and thus allowing your body to utilise the energy it would otherwise expend on fear. Then, when I pinpoint the reason for my fear, I realise that it is Barnie; Barnie for whom I fear should anything happen to me. And isn't it a mother's role to protect her child? If I'm gone, who will protect Barnie? I know there are plenty of people who would, but that's not the issue. The point is that I cannot ignore maternal instincts.

What I can do is find a place for the fear, so that every time I see the scars (both physical and mental), or have a pain, or attend a check-up, I acknowledge that fear and do not blame myself for it. Slowly, as each check-up is clear and each pain inconsequential, the fear will diminish... but then, who knows, perhaps there will be another one. Like the fact that we cannot always be happy, and have to accept black times as well as good times, we cannot always be free of fear; fear of spiders, the dark, driving alone, being ridiculed, flying, cancer. How precious life is with its ups and downs. Quotes and credos fly through my head now; 'Carpe diem,' (seize the day), 'Whatever you can do, or dream you can... begin it' (Goethe), 'What you put into life, you get out of it' (my mother!), 'With all its sham, drudgery and broken dreams, it is still a beautiful world. Be cheerful, strive to be happy' (Desiderata). Credos are no good if you are not first happy in your own shell. Oh for the number of mornings when I woke with fresh words and resolutions on my lips, with the promise to be happy, to seize the day. And how quickly were they dashed time and again by the sheer drudgery of getting myself through the day. Such resolutions sat at the top of a sheer sided, ladder-less well in which I sat. Time and patience and forcing myself to go straight through the door finally enabled me to climb the well and seize the words which brought about this trip. I thank God and the world that I am here now, at the end of this dead end road, in the dripping rain, alone except for a sleeping Barnie, a sleeping Tess and an invisible Ben.

I can hear an owl, then an oystercatcher calls shrilly through the dark. I love to hear the oystercatchers. They used to fly with such urgency above and around me when walking the coast that I often thought they were trying to tell me something. They were especially urgent when we reached the Thames at the end, as were all the birds. The turnstones, curlew, redshank, shelduck and every other bird flew in such a fanfare over the last few days that I was convinced they knew. This time, the birds have been absent. There has been the odd raptor and redwing, but nothing like the array of waders on the coast. It is appropriate to be reassured by a vocal but invisible oystercatcher tonight.

I am sitting at the entrance of the tent, watching the rain drops fall off the canvas flap by torchlight and smoking a damp rollie. Rob has had to go back to be in time for work in the morning. It is a lonely and unceremonious ending, but my mind is full, so full, of everything that has happened and of an enormous resolution. I know it will probably be dashed tomorrow, but who cares? We are all fallible.

No Horse to Take Home

Monday 30 September

The silence this morning was familiar. Or was it a sixth sense which told me that Ben wasn't within five hundred yards of us, where he should have been? I have developed an intuition with Ben which mothers will be familiar with; I just knew things weren't right.

Bundling Barnie on to my back, we made a quick first search of the field. All that was achieved was that Barnie lost a welly at the bottom of the hill in the long grass and I had to retrace my steps, cursing, to find it. My thin temper reminded me that, horse or no horse, we needed food. I shovelled powdered milk and muesli down Barnie and me, not tasting or enjoying, just fuelling a pair of empty tanks, then set off after Ben properly. I have walked miles this morning after that frustrating but loveable horse; the morning when I envisaged waking leisurely and musing away the hours until Virginia arrived. He was in a burn-side field and had simply wandered up the burn in search of another Ben adventure. The adventure had culminated in a vertical climb to a fenced-in precipice. I found him hemmed in on one side by a new wire fence and the other by this vertical drop littered with hock breaking boulders and rusty wire.

Dumping Barnie in his back pack in the neighbouring field, I tried coaxing Ben back down the precipice. I hung from his rope and looked up to his vast frame, hoping yet not hoping that he would leap, and wondering who would find Barnie in his backpack if both Ben and I ended up in a heap at the bottom of the cliff. Wise Ben wouldn't budge an inch, illustrating that what goes up doesn't necessarily come down. Realising that the only option was to cut the wire, we walked back to the farm. Dick and the boss were away for the morning and we had several hours to kill before they returned. Dick's wife, Marjorie, had soon taken us in and fed us toast, while Barnie insisted on sweeping the floor with the scrubbing brush and feeding the washing machine with pieces of toast and the bristly broom head.

When Virginia arrived at midday there was still no horse to load into the trailer. I hoped and presumed that I still had a horse standing quietly on a narrow ledge, calm because of the proximity of some cattle and waiting for good ol' mum to come and rescue him. Sure enough, when I drove back in a Land Rover with Dick and the boss, a white blaze and pair of brown ears looked up to welcome our arrival. We cut him out easily and I climbed on to him and walked him back, the final homecoming. I thought, then, how much I was looking forward to going 'home' – to the luxuries which had been absent for three weeks, and the thought of the deepest sleep. Yet I also felt anxious about the homecoming.

Anxious about facing the 'real' world once more, and sad that life on the road would end again.

It would be easy to say that everything has changed now; that I am walking home into the sunset, philosophical and fully accepting of the cancer and its legacy. I never was very good at lying (besides, there aren't too many sunsets in Scotland at this time of year). Instead, it is a murky horizon which beckons. There is nothing definite about the margin between earth and sky, nothing definite about the future except that it is inevitable. But I am going home with a peace which I can now see was so missing in the mayhem of the last year. I may have spent a good part of the previous year sitting still physically, but I never sat still in my head. My head churned with its cocktail of thoughts and fears and unanswered questions; now I have walked and felt calm again.

Life After the Drove

Things don't just stop. As long as the earth rotates, gravity holds us down, and there are a few forests left to provide us with oxygen, (and 'The Archers' exists), we will go on living, laughing and suffering. 'And they all lived happily ever after,' would be a boring scenario anyway. How much richer life is for the problems it throws at us, the opportunities it offers through the various crises. Yet why is it that our society preaches, through advertising and media, that everyone should be happy? It guides us down the path of false illusion which makes us think, when something goes wrong, that life has somehow dealt us a bad hand. Life is life, hard with soft and tender parts – those are the times to cherish, the parts which enable us to see blue sky among dark clouds.

Two weeks after the drove I had my three-monthly check-up and was given the all-clear. A month later I developed an abdominal pain which persisted and persisted. As I sat writing this book over the winter of the following year, transcribing from my dictaphone and referring to diaries and memories, fear set in again. What was this pain? Was the man back in the dark room wielding his sharp knife?

Despite the fact that the doctors assured me the pain was nothing suspicious, fear threatened rationality. Then someone reminded me to read my own words. I flicked back through my endless jottings and the book as it was taking form, and was comforted by the fact that I had found peace, perspective and a place for fear once. Somewhere out there, possibly around the next corner or the next, I could find that equilibrium again. Still, it is hard to be ever philosophical when you are uncomfortable.

Later, much later, after several periods of tear-inducing pain and nights spent musing on what on earth was wrong now, a test revealed that the abdominal pain resulted partly from a lactose intolerance. I went off dairy products and for a while felt better than I had done for years. Funny, really, that one of the reasons I felt so well during the Grampian trip was that we ate hardly any dairy products. It was the lavish western diet I resumed which made me feel so awful.

There are many diets recommended to prevent cancer; potential carcinogens appear with regularity, depending on the latest scientific finding. There is too much to do in the world without chasing contradictory health fads. I am not prepared to wrap myself in cotton wool and sharpen my teeth on carrots for the rest of my life. However, one theory suggests that dairy products feed cancer. In a strange way, the fact that my body rejected dairy products renewed my faith in it; as though it had woken from its stunned slumber and illustrated that it had a voice again.

If physical travel is tiring, emotional travel is more so. Body and soul must be allowed time to re-group after trauma;

some people meditate, others lie in the bath, others work in the garden or sing, some walk. One thing is certain – you cannot ignore the traumatic effects of such travel. They say that time is the healer but I say that you are the healer and time is your friend. Going straight through the door is hard, but so much easier than waiting for time.

Meanwhile, Barnie stomped about the house in true toddler form. He threw impressive tantrums, but was usually pacified by anything horsey. Calling him horse mad was an understatement. He climbed aboard anything which could possibly resemble a horse (Tess lying down, the arm of the sofa, the sewing machine, Rob's canoe lying outside, Rob or me lying down), grabbed imaginary reins, and clicked his tongue while bouncing up and down. If he doesn't ride around Aintree one day, I thought, it will only be because height and weight prevent him. His return to four solid walls after the trip wasn't easy. If the door looked like being opened, he was out like a shot and could usually only be diverted with a copy of *Horse & Hound* magazine. Persuading him that we weren't going to eat lunch on the muddy grass in the howling wind wasn't so easy.

Tess was delighted to be back in the warmth and comfort of a house. The ripped dew claw had to be removed, and she pottered around with a large bandage on for a few days, milking sympathy dry. Ben had a well-deserved rest. He replaced the weight lost in the Highlands, and revelled in the fences which enclosed him and the fact that he had a water trough from which he could drink at will. No more sporadic peaty burns for the urban horse.

In February, Ben's rest came to an end. Barnie was delighted to be back in the saddle and it sometimes seemed that the two of them communicated at a far deeper level than I could ever understand. Both were unaware that Ben was soon to become our mode of transport. The perfect horse drawn cart was been found. A summer project.

So I sat in April '98, looking out over brave but dejected daffodils fooled into early flowering by uncharacteristic warmth, only to be rudely flattened by snow. The geese left, leaving a strange silence in their wake. The seed fields which were full of their chatter grew fast, and very soon the first swallows appeared. Spring may not always be warm, but its arrival is one of life's few certainties.

When Borders' weather allowed, Barnie and I sat out in our wilderness garden alongside a tall and healthy oak sapling – the acorn which symbolised Barnie's conception in Devon and which accompanied us ever since. Barnie was only likely to sit still if there were tractors working in the field below, or lorries speeding noiselessly along the distant road. I used to watch his little face, so intent until toddler restlessness set in and he was off exploring again, and wonder whether it was possible to love him any more than I did. *One day,* I thought, *I'll fulfil my promise and take him swimming with dolphins.*

Epilogue

December 2009

Barnie is now thirteen and prefers mountain bikes to horses!

In 1999 Rob and I were married, and Rob adopted Barnie. We then adopted a little brother for Barnie, JP, who is now seven and gorgeous like his brother.

Sadly Tess died and her passing left a huge hole in my life. But I still have Ben who pulls a cart, and we have had lots of fun with him. He is still lazy and needs constant encouragement to go forwards!

Healthwise, the abdominal pain I suffered was not quite so simply cured. It turned out to be scarring from the operation and I have suffered with this pain, off and on for years. Chronic pain is exhausting but somehow you learn to live with it.

More importantly, I am once again suffering from cancer. Two years ago I was diagnosed with lung cancer. I had smoked rollies for years but never heavily. Apparently, I have a susceptibility to cancer.

The cancer has now spread to my brain and my bones. I have treatment regularly, radiotherapy and chemotherapy, to try and keep it at bay, and I am as determined as anything. Maternal instinct is very strong at times like this – my boys keep me going, as does the almost self-sufficient smallholding I run here in the Borders. A week ago we had seven piglets; I need a tup for our five ewes and five of last year's lambs need slaughtering. The vegetable garden needs working for next year and we have lots of tree planting planned.

I do not want to leave this life because there is still too much to do and besides, I am having far too much fun.

Appendix

Cervical Cancer – the facts

• Regular screening for cervical cancer began in 1988 and since then the death rate from this cancer has been steadily falling. I was a success story of the screening programme.

• It is recommended that smears should be performed on women between the ages of fifteen and sixty-four every three years (a *minimum* of every five years).

• The smear test is designed to pick up any changes in cells in the cervix which *might* become cancerous if not treated. My case was unusual because cervical cancer usually takes many years to develop. If you have regular smears, any abnormality is likely to be picked up at an early stage, and treated.

• Of smears performed, 95% are negative, 4.5% are borderline and will be repeated, and only 0.5% are positive. Those that are positive will be looked at more closely by colposcopy (microscopic examination of the cervix).

• The abnormalities range from mild to severe; some are found to be a result of post-natal changes in the cervix, or viral infections, while others may be pre-cancerous and can be successfully treated at colposcopy. Of the 0.5% positive, only a 'very, very small number' are full-blown cancer.

• Unfortunately, only 85% of woman attend their smears. If you are one of those 15% who don't, you're mad. GO NOW!

Postscript

Sadly, Spud died on 14 January 2010 at home, surrounded by her family. She remained courageous and determined to the end, an inspiration to us all in death as she was in life; a truly exceptional mother, wife, sister, aunt, godmother and friend to so many.

This book and *Two Feet, Four Paws* form part of an impressive legacy. The very personal nature of Spud's writings gives you an insight into the wonderful woman she was.

Her funeral, at her request, was a colourful affair. Many have commented how they were moved and at times uplifted by the readings, hymns and eulogies. Many promised to walk more and generally do more with their lives, impressed by the amount Spud had packed into hers. So we were all able to take something positive from this unique occasion; I know she would have approved.

Rob Cutting, February 2010

Bibliography

Haldane, A. R. B., *The Drove Roads of Scotland* (1997, Birlinn, Edinburgh)

Bonser, J. K., *The Drovers: Who They Were and How They Went* (1970, Macmillan, London)

Have you enjoyed this book? If so, why not write a review
on your favourite website?

Thanks very much for buying this Summersdale book.

www.summersdale.com